A Conver

A CONVERSATION WITH WISDOM

BY
DR. JOSEPH N. WILLIAMS
EDITED BY EBONY MURDOCH

TRUE PERSPECTIVE PUBLISHING HOUSE

A Conversation with Wisdom

A Conversation with Wisdom

Copyright © 2011 by Dr. Joseph N. Williams
A Conversation with Wisdom

Printed in the United States of America

ISBN 978-0-9832399-7-0

All rights reserved solely by the author. The author guarantees all contents are original and do not infringe upon the legal rights of any other person or work. No part of this book may be reproduced in any form without the permission of the author. The views expressed in this book are not necessarily those of the publisher.

King James Version
Public Domain in America
New King James Version®
Copyright © 1982 by Thomas Nelson, Inc. All rights reserved

www.trueperspectivepublishing.com

A Conversation with Wisdom

A Conversation with Wisdom

ACKNOWLEDGEMENTS

I want to first acknowledge God, in whose favor and blessings I live daily and have been given another privilege to advance His Kingdom through this endeavor.

To my wife Carolyn, for giving me the time and freedom to accomplish such a task, thank you! Your support and encouragement over the years, has been a blessing and an invaluable contribution to my life. I Love You.

To Mrs. Ebony E. Murdoch, whose understanding, time and patience, unraveled lessons, scattered notes and anecdotal material into a workable format. Your personal touch, creativity and editing has encouraged me in the publishing process. May God grant "abundant blessings" on your life. Thank You!

To the scores of sons and daughters, who attended these teachings, exercising the principles of wisdom taught and fulfilling the call of God upon their lives. Thank You!

To the ministry of helps in those behind the scene needs: Adrienne Height, Carl Wauchope, Keiron Phillips, Verania Kenton. Thank You!

A Conversation with Wisdom

To my mentor, Bishop Edward E. Williams, who's paternal concern and affection has allowed me to grow and mature. Those "nuggets" of wisdom are priceless. Thank You!

To my son in Christ, Sean Cort, whose "Power of Perspective" has motivated and mobilized this project into a reality. Thank You!

Dr. Joseph N. Williams, Sr.

Additional Info/Credits:
Photography: CedricWooten.Carbonmade.com
Imaging: Malluda Productions
Promo Edits: DlakeMedia.com

A Conversation with Wisdom

AUTOGRAPH PAGE

A Conversation with Wisdom

A Conversation with Wisdom

PREFACE

WISDOM IS ABOUT DOING BUSINESS GOD'S WAY

The kingdom of God, which is the sphere of influence in which God is the sovereign ruler, is primarily about doing business God's way. This kingdom does not come with observation, but exists within true gospel believers (corporately and individually), manifesting itself in righteousness, peace, and joy in the Holy Ghost. When we walk uprightly, we adorn the gospel, making Christ attractive to others. So it's critical that we live and move in step with kingdom principles-for the advancement of God's purposes and fulfillment of our destinies. What better way to do this than to pursue His wisdom with humble, worshipful hearts?

Through diligent study of the principles of godly wisdom, your mind will be renewed and transformed. God's wisdom is everywhere-in the multiplicity of the stars and in the paying of our rent. It's in the layout of the visible universe— it's in the way we speak to one another. It's in the plan of our salvation, and in the choices we make each day. No wonder the Bible declares, "Wisdom is the principal thing, and in all thy getting, get an understanding" (Prov. 4:7).

It's time to dialogue with your destiny and increase the level of God's wisdom in your life. If you are wise, you will hear, and increase in learning-if you have understanding, you will attain to wise counsels (Prov. 1:5). The indwelling Spirit will empower us to carry out the decrees of the Kingdom as we believe God's word and yield to His work within us.

A Conversation with Wisdom

A Conversation with Wisdom

INTRODUCTION

FROM THE HEART OF THE FATHER

A new season of change is taking place all around us, particularly in the political and economic arenas. Because all truth is parallel, changes in the natural realm are a signal to the Body of Christ that something is happening in the spiritual realm. God wants us to have a full understanding of why He called us and how our assignments must be carried out. To attain this, we must receive and observe His wisdom. Regression is never an option: you will never go forward until you decide that you are not going backward. The words of Apostle Paul are still a challenge:

Brethren, I count not myself yet to have laid hold: but one thing I do, forgetting the things which are behind, and stretching forward to the things which are before, I press on toward the goal unto the prize of the high calling of God in Christ Jesus. (Php 3:13-14 ASV)

God has called us to be a peculiar people. He calls us to understand that He is never lacking in spiritual or natural riches. I proclaim to you it's time for an elevation of your faith. It's time to do things differently-wisely and with passion. I encourage each of you to remain focused on the word, worship and warfare in these unprecedented times.

Bishop Joseph Nathaniel Williams,
Pastor & Founder, Christ Church International
Jamaica, New York

A Conversation with Wisdom

A Conversation with Wisdom

TABLE OF CONTENTS

FOREWARD...xv

CHAPTER ONE
What is Wisdom?..17

CHAPTER TWO
Wisdom Personified...13

CHAPTER THREE
Four Types of Fools..43

CHAPTER FOUR
Proverbs: Choosing What's Better.....................................53

CHAPTER FIVE
Setting and Maintaining Wise Boundaries.........................67

CHAPTER SIX
Wisdom @ Work..77

CHAPTER SEVEN
Ecclesiastes: The Search for Life's Meaning.....................91

A Conversation with Wisdom

CHAPTER EIGHT

Principles of Financial Wisdom..............................99

CHAPTER NINE

How to Determine the Right Course of Action.............111

CHAPTER TEN

Selecting Your Cabinet..125

CHAPTER ELEVEN

Linking Our Goals to God's Purpose.....................131

CHAPTER TWELVE

The Art of Speaking Wisely...................................135

CHAPTER THIRTEEN

Making It Personal..143

RECOMMENDED READING...............................149

A Conversation with Wisdom

FOREWARD

We live in a time where information is available to us on any subject, or about anything. This information is easily accessible particularly on the internet, but also in books, theatres, television, and on the streets. The age of informaniacs does reign and rule in our culture. CNN, Fox News and other media stations feed the public with an overwhelming amount of global, national and local events. It seems as if the more we know it is the more we desire to know.

The church seemingly has played its part in the dissemination of so-called biblical information. Our religious stations are available to us 24/7. Each telecast or broadcast pour out their thoughts, feelings and interpretations as to what Christians should know and what Christians should do. Yet, people are desperate for truth and starving for guidance.

This book with its handbook will give clear and concise explanation concerning the wisdom of God. There are many wisdom teachers and gurus in our culture, yet no other wisdom can connect us with our creator and our eternal destiny, but the wisdom that is from above. Where is this wisdom found? It is carefully placed throughout the Bible and can be discovered by diligent study and consistent application.

I encourage you to take this book as one of your keys to unlock the doors of God's divine principles for living a life pleasing to Him. Share it with your family, friends and neighbors and watch the wisdom, purpose and plan of God increase in the lives of those who embrace it. This is the season to get closer to God, learn His way and grow in His life. This book will move you to know God and become His true disciple.

Submitted by: Rev. Dr. Jacqueline McCullough,
Senior Pastor of The International Gathering at Beth Rapha
Pomona, New York

A Conversation with Wisdom

Wisdom is the principal thing; therefore get wisdom; yea, with all thy getting get an understanding.
Proverbs 4:7

Who is as the wise man? and who knoweth the interpretation of a thing? A man's wisdom maketh his face to shine, and the hardness of his face is changed.
King Solomon

CHAPTER ONE

INTRODUCTION TO WISDOM

1.1 WHAT'S IN A WORD?

In today's vernacular, wisdom is generally associated with knowing what course of action to take in a given situation, usually of some difficulty. However, when it comes to recognizing and implementing specific principles of biblical wisdom, many of us come up short. One of the goals of this chapter is to provide a comprehensive way of looking at wisdom that will enable us to think about and face life's daily challenges in positive ways. On this journey, we will find that

A Conversation with Wisdom

there is a lot more to wisdom than meets the eye, and that the Lord has graciously inspired short, succinct answers to our most pressing concerns in the pages of scripture.

According to *Vine's Expository Dictionary of Old and New Testament Words*, the ancient Hebrews thought of wisdom in terms of its relationship to skill or mastery. The Hebrew word *hakam* referred to the art of living in obedience to God, something that had to be mastered over the course of a lifetime. The noun form of the word "wisdom" is *hokmah*. While this can refer to skill in making things (i.e., tabernacle furniture, priestly garments), it also indicates the ability to make the right choices at the right time based on the fear of the Lord.

The pursuit of wisdom edifies and strengthens the Body of Christ, and advances the interests of the Kingdom of God. The kingdom of God is a realm of spiritual life that one can only see or enter by way of the new birth (John 3:3, 5). In this sphere, God is the sovereign, and business-all business-must be done His way. He has given us the Holy Ghost (the Spirit of Wisdom) to help us in our Christian walk. God calls us to "become" through wise instruction what He designed us to "be," because we will never *be* what we have not *become*.

A person does not have to be advanced in years to pursue true, godly wisdom. In fact, many biblical calls to wisdom are addressed specifically to the young. One thing is certain, however. We must be *passionate* in our pursuit of wisdom. We must be *willing* to embrace radical changes in the way we think, which is another way of saying "be ye transformed by the renewing of your mind" (Romans 12:2). Wisdom does not come for the purpose of increasing intellectual knowledge, but to offer practical instruction that will profoundly affect the hearts of those who receive it. Do you have a heart to receive wisdom from the Lord today (Pro. 22:17-19)?

A Conversation with Wisdom

THE FIRST STEP TOWARD WISDOM IS THE FEAR OF THE LORD

> *The fear of the LORD is the beginning of knowledge; But the foolish despise wisdom and instruction. (Pro. 1:7)*

The fear of the Lord does not indicate terror or fright, as from something monstrous that is about to inflict harm, but rather deep reverence, as to a person of great respect and authority. The more we recognize the greatness of God and His authority over the minutest details of our everyday lives; the more our lifestyle will reflect this reverence. We will not want to grieve the Spirit by acting in ways contrary to His will-and if we do, we will be quick to repent-turning away completely from evil ideologies and practices. Joseph demonstrated the fear of the Lord when he fled from Potiphar's lustful wife, leaving his garment in her hand. "How can I do this great wickedness," he asked, "and sin against God?" (Gen 39:9) His responded wisely in the midst of temptation (1 Cor. 10:13; 1 Jn. 2:16).

The first human confrontation on the nature and value of wisdom occurred during the Dispensation of Innocence, when Satan tempted Eve by questioning the goodness of God in forbidding them to eat from the Tree of the Knowledge of Good and Evil (Gen. 3:1-5). It was the first time man sought to acquire wisdom apart from the wisdom of God, with dramatic and dire consequences. Eve did not yet realize the truth declared in Proverbs 21:30: "[There is] no wisdom, nor understanding, nor counsel against the LORD."

> *And the serpent said unto the woman, Ye shall not surely die: For God doth know that in the day ye eat thereof, then your eyes shall be opened, and ye shall be as gods, knowing good and evil. And when the woman saw that the tree [was] good for food, and that it [was] pleasant*

A Conversation with Wisdom

*to the eyes, and **a tree to be desired to make [one] wise**, she took of the fruit thereof, and did eat, and gave also unto her husband with her; and he did eat. (Gen. 3:4-6)*

The Hebrew words for "to make [one] wise" is *sakal*, which means among other things "to have insight or comprehension" or "to cause to prosper." It is as if Satan said, "Listen, Eve. You're not going to die. God is holding out on you. Life can be even better for you than you think. He just doesn't want you to know what He knows or to be like Him. Once your eyes are opened, then you'll really be wise." Sadly, this kind of reasoning about God and true wisdom persists to this day. It is dangerous to reject the clear word of the Lord in exchange for the promise of superior wisdom or well-being from another place. As the saying goes, we must "consider the source."

1.2 WISDOM LITERATURE

This workbook focuses on various teachings about wisdom taken primarily from the books of Proverbs and Ecclesiastes. However, dozens of cross references to scriptures in other books are included in order to provide a broader view of the subject matter. Proverbs, Ecclesiastes Job, and certain Psalms comprise what theologians refer to as "wisdom literature."

The book of Proverbs is a collection of wise sayings written or transcribed by different authors, including King Solomon, Agur, and King Lemuel. Solomon is credited with being the main author. He spoke 3,000 proverbs in his lifetime (I Ki. 4:32). Proverbs is comprised of direct instruction (i.e., a father to his son), parallelism (a comparison or contrasting of two or more ideas), and the acrostic poem, used in chapter 31 to describe the Virtuous Woman.

The book of Ecclesiastes was written by Solomon, who is called *Qoheleth*, or, "the Preacher." Here, he presents a

A Conversation with Wisdom

series of philosophical arguments on the meaning of life and tries to make sense of the ironies that fill it. The book about life "under the sun," or the earthly, human viewpoint on our existence. The fear of God is seen in Ecclesiastes as "the conclusion of the matter," whereas in Proverbs, the fear of the Lord is the "beginning of wisdom" (Eccl. 12:13; Pro. 9:10). Like Proverbs, it features sharp contrasts between the wise and the foolish.

KING SOLOMON ASKED FOR WISDOM...BUT GREATER THAN SOLOMON IS HERE

Solomon recognized the importance of wisdom when he was given the opportunity to ask for anything he wanted from the LORD. Instead of asking for wealth, fame, or the execution of his enemies, he requested wisdom and *discernment* to help in the governance of God's people (1 Kings 3:9). His request for wisdom occurred between two acts of extravagant worship, in which he offered burnt offerings and peace offerings to God (I Kings 3:4-5, 15). The impartation of wisdom Solomon received from the Lord was first demonstrated by solving a difficult child custody battle between two prostitutes (1 Kings 3:16-27). This led to the fame of his wisdom being spread abroad:

> *And all Israel heard of the judgment that the king had rendered, and they stood in awe of the king, because they perceived that the wisdom of God was in him to do justice. (1 Kings 3:28)*

Dignitaries, like the Queen of Sheba, traveled great distances just to hear his wisdom. Because of his sharpened discernment, he was able to disclose to her all the questions of her mind and heart. She was so overwhelmed by this, his wealth, the attire of his servants, and his access to the house of God, that she literally passed out (1 Kings 10:1-10). In Luke 11:31, Jesus spoke of this woman, saying she would rise to

A Conversation with Wisdom

judge His generation-because One "greater than Solomon is here," and they were unable to recognize this and turn to Him.

Solomon was one of the wisest men who ever lived, and yet the greatest example of wisdom in action can be found in the Son of God, of whom it was said when He was a child,

> *And Jesus increased in **wisdom** and in **stature** and in **favor** with God and man. (Luke 2:52)*

A careful reading of the life and ministry of our Lord will show that He walked in perfect balance at all times. He was always in fellowship with the Father. He knew when it was time to speak, and when it was better to say nothing. He radiated wisdom by walking in appropriate emotional responses to external situations, and although tempted in all points as we are, He did not sin (Heb. 4:15). In so doing, He showed us not only the power of God, but the wisdom of God as it plays out in daily life. Wisdom is stabilizing-it keeps a person from walking in unhealthy extremes (Eccl. 7:18, NIV).

Wisdom is connected to the word, to worship, and to spiritual warfare (the bringing down of anything that exalts itself against the knowledge of God). It is also linked to the favor of God upon a life. People often quote the verse which says, "whoso findeth a wife findeth a good thing, and obtaineth favor of the LORD" (Pro. 18:22), but a similar statement is made about wisdom, and the benefit is not just a good thing, but life itself, in its qualitative sense.

> *For whoso findeth me [Wisdom] findeth life, and shall obtain favor of the LORD. (Pro. 8:35)*

1.3 DIVINE WISDOM

GOD USED WISDOM IN ACTS OF CREATION AND THE PLAN OF REDEMPTION

On three occasions in the New Testament, we are told that the Lord is the "only wise God," and that this wisdom is

A Conversation with Wisdom

commensurate with His greatness (Rom. 16:27; 1 Tim. 1:17 and Jud. 25). He founded the universe through wisdom (Pro. 3:19). This same wisdom devised the plan of redemption through the death of the Lord Jesus (1 Cor. 2:7-8). Paul could barely describe the magnitude of this divine attribute, and he could only say, "O the depth of the riches both of the wisdom and knowledge of God! How unsearchable [are] his judgments, and his ways past finding out!" (Rom. 11:33) Christ was made unto us the very wisdom of God (1 Cor. 1:30) The Holy Ghost is called the "Spirit of Wisdom" in Isaiah 11:2, a designation clearly manifested in the life and ministry of Christ. The Holy Ghost also distributes the spiritual gift of wisdom to those whom He wills in the Body of Christ (1 Cor. 12:7-8,11).

When Moses spoke to the children of Israel about the importance of obedience and keeping the statutes and testimonies of the LORD, he said,

> *Keep them and do them, for that will be your wisdom and your understanding in the sight of the peoples, who, when they hear all these statues will say, 'Surely this great nation is a wise and understanding people.'" (Deut. 4:6, ESV)*

Likewise, when we walk in the commandments of Christ, others should be able to perceive His wisdom in us. It is a contradiction of our profession not to behave wisely in our daily affairs (Col. 4:5). Wisdom enables us to navigate the rough terrain of life with skill and precision. It involves a maturation process, just as all other graces and spiritual disciplines. Yet if we continue in faith and obedience, we will be able to stand and withstand whatever comes against us. Jesus said:

> *Every one therefore that <u>heareth</u> these words of mine, and <u>doeth</u> them, shall be likened unto a **wise** man, who built his house upon the rock:*

*and the rain descended, and the floods came,
and the winds blew, and beat upon that house;
and it fell not: for it was founded upon the rock.
(Mat. 7:24-25, ASV)*

1.4 HOW TO OBTAIN WISDOM
PRAYER AND PROMISES RELEASE WISDOM

So far, we have learned that wisdom involves skill and mastery over a lifetime; that it is rooted in deep reverence for the Lord; and that it leads into a life of growth, prosperity, and balance in every area of life. We have looked at Solomon and how extraordinary wisdom manifested itself in wise judgment; and at the broad-sweeping wisdom of God in creation and redemption. So now that we know what it is, the question remains, *how do we get it?*

Wisdom is necessary for a life that pleases God - it is not an option! According to the apostle James, wisdom is available for the asking, but it must be sought for in faith (Jas. 1:5-6). This means arriving a place where we can admit to the Lord our lack of wisdom, whether it be in a specific test/trial/temptation or in a broader sense of the ways we manage our time, speak to others, deal with anger, or handle our finances. We are encouraged to apply these proverbs and pithy sayings to our lives for maximum benefit, and to pass these instructions down to the next generation. Wisdom is priceless, worth more than jewels or any other material thing we may desire (Pro. 3:15; Eccl. 7:12). Why? Because wisdom enriches the lives of those who possess it with general blessing, long life, peace, durable wealth, honor, fearlessness/boldness, and security about their destinies (Pro. 3:16-26).

The wisdom of God can be granted by promise or divine decree for special circumstances, as it was to the early Christians. The Lord Jesus stated during His earthly ministry that His disciples should not worry about how to answer their critics, for He would give them "a mouth and wisdom which all your adversaries will not be able to gainsay or resist" (Luk.

21:14-15). This promise was fulfilled as the saints faced persecution for the faith-and it is available for us today as well.

> *And Stephen, full of grace and power, wrought great wonders and signs among the people. But there arose certain of them that were of the synagogue called the synagogue of the Libertines, and of the Cyrenians, and of the Alexandrians, and of them of Cilicia and Asia, disputing with Stephen. And they were not able to withstand the wisdom and the Spirit by which he spake. (Act 6:8-10 ASV)*

Note that the fullness and power of the Holy Ghost works in conjunction with the expression of wisdom in the midst of conflict and challenge. To be full of the Spirit is to be full of God-and all the attributes that make Him who He is-including His wisdom.

TYPES OF WISDOM

There are different kinds of wisdom. They may be identified by the sources from which they spring; but as well as by their fruit. Consider that true wisdom will impact the thoughts, words, characters and behavior of those who live by it. James' teaching provides us with some firm guidelines as to what constitutes true wisdom.

> *Who is wise and understanding among you? let him show by his good life his works in meekness of wisdom. But if ye have bitter jealousy and faction in your heart, glory not and lie not against the truth.* ***This wisdom is not a wisdom that cometh down from above****, but is earthly, sensual, devilish. For where jealousy and faction are, there is confusion and every vile deed. But **the wisdom that is from above** is first*

A Conversation with Wisdom

pure, then peaceable, gentle, easy to be entreated, full of mercy and good fruits, without variance, without hypocrisy. And the fruit of righteousness is sown in peace for them that make peace. (Jas 3:13-18 ASV)

Note that wisdom bears good fruit. Are you bearing this good fruit today? Are you pure, peaceful, gentle, easy to speak to? How about full of mercy? Are you the same person all the time, or do you change depending on who is looking? Consider these questions as we press through this workbook. Take them up in prayer, and ask the Lord for wisdom-He will give it to you liberally-and without rebuke (Jas. 1:5).

1.4.1　　EXERCISE

Read Proverbs 1:1-7. Write two paragraphs explaining the purposes of this biblical book as stated in those verses. What do you learn about the role of wisdom and instruction in a life devoted to God's glory each day? What do you expect to gain from this series?

1.4.2　　EXERCISE

Review James 3:13-18 and identify the sevenfold nature of heavenly wisdom. Commit this list to memory.

[Teacher's Notes: 1) Discuss the story of Solomon's request for wisdom in more detail, in particular the concept that worship encounters often lead to the release of information to aid the worshipper in their current or next assignment; 2) Discuss the role of wise men in the courts of biblical kings and leaders, in particular those who manipulated others through divination. Highlight special occasions when God allowed righteous men, such as Daniel and Joseph, to interpret dreams or give well-timed prophetic guidance to leaders, resulting in the salvation of lives. You may also want to note that wise

A Conversation with Wisdom

men, called *magos,* visited the Child Jesus after following His star in the east (Mat. 2:1-2); 3) Explain that this section covers advanced theological themes in a brief, general manner. Students interested in further study may refer to the "Resources to Help You Section"; and 4) Expand on the connection between the power of the Holy Ghost and the expression of wisdom, particularly in times of conflict. Discuss it from the perspective of front-line apologetics (defending the faith), as well as daily dealings with personal enemies. Explain that for something as simple as serving widows in the daily allowance, anointing and wisdom were required (Acts 6:3).]

A Conversation with Wisdom

A Conversation with Wisdom

Because the foolishness of God is wiser than men; and the weakness of God is stronger than men.
Paul the Apostle

CHAPTER TWO

WISDOM PERSONIFIED

2.1 WISDOM HAS A VOICE

*I*n the literary technique known as personification, the writer ascribes human characteristics to an object, idea, or other non-living thing. Under the inspiration of the Spirit, King Solomon presents wisdom to readers of Scripture in the form of a woman pleading with the public to heed her words (Eccl. 12:10; 2 Pet. 1:21). Later in the book, he uses the same technique to present Folly. The voice of the LORD is evident in the midst of these entreaties, for Christ Himself is the wisdom of God (Pro. 8:22-36; 1 Cor. 1:24).

Scripture also attributes dialogue to the adulteress and paints a portrait of the virtuous woman, whose life is characterized by wisdom and the fear of the Lord. While chapter 31 is not written in first person, it has served as a model for godly women across the centuries, whether they

A Conversation with Wisdom

married and raised children or were singularly devoted to the service of Christ. By presenting these attributes in the form of a personal narrative, Solomon arrests our attention with straightforward encouragement and warning.

2.2 WISDOM - FIRST SPEECH

In this passage, wisdom is likened to a woman crying out to pedestrians as they go on their ways in the city streets. Wisdom pleads earnestly with men, as they continue to oppose God's righteous authority, to repent of their folly while there is still time. It is dangerous for a man not to receive the fear of the Lord and to despise His reproofs. In the final analysis, their own "backsliding" and "careless ease" will be the cause of their destruction.

> *Wisdom crieth aloud in the street; She uttereth her voice in the broad places; She crieth in the chief place of concourse; At the entrance of the gates, In the city, she uttereth her words: How long, ye simple ones, will ye love simplicity? And scoffers delight them in scoffing, And fools hate knowledge? Turn you at my reproof: Behold, I will pour out my spirit upon you; I will make known my words unto you. Because I have called, and ye have refused; I have stretched out my hand, and no man hath regarded; But ye have set at nought all my counsel, And would none of my reproof: I also will laugh in the day of your calamity; I will mock when your fear cometh; When your fear cometh as a storm, And your calamity cometh on as a whirlwind; When distress and anguish come upon you. Then will they call upon me, but I will not answer; They will seek me diligently, but they shall not find me: For that they hated knowledge, And did not*

choose the fear of Jehovah: They would none of my counsel; They despised all my reproof. Therefore shall they eat of the fruit of their own way, And be filled with their own devices. For the backsliding of the simple shall slay them, And the careless ease of fools shall destroy them. **But whoso hearkeneth unto me shall dwell securely, And shall be quiet without fear of evil.** *(Proverbs 1:20-33)*

2.2.1   EXERCISE

What are your thoughts on this passage? What is the result of despising knowledge and instruction? Why is it so terrible to be left to one's own devices? Write a brief response to this passage and commit verse 33 to memory. Be prepared to recite it for the next class.

2.3 WISDOM- SECOND SPEECH

Beside the gates, at the entry of the city, At the coming in at the doors, she [Wisdom] crieth aloud: Unto you, O men, I call; And my voice is to the sons of men. O ye simple, understand prudence; And, ye fools, be of an understanding heart. Hear, for I will speak excellent things; And the opening of my lips shall be right things. For my mouth shall utter truth; And wickedness is an abomination to my lips. All the words of my mouth are in righteousness; There is nothing crooked or perverse in them. They are all plain to him that understandeth, And right to them that find knowledge. **Receive my instruction, and not silver; And knowledge rather than choice gold. For wisdom is better than rubies; And all the things that may be desired are not to be compared unto it.** *I Wisdom have made*

A Conversation with Wisdom

prudence my dwelling, And find out knowledge and discretion. **The fear of Jehovah is to hate evil: Pride, and arrogancy, and the evil way, And the perverse mouth, do I hate. Counsel is mine, and sound knowledge: I am understanding; I have might.** *By me kings reign, And princes decree justice. By me princes rule, And nobles, even all the judges of the earth. I love them that love me; And those that seek me diligently shall find me. Riches and honor are with me; Yea, durable wealth and righteousness. My fruit is better than gold, yea, than fine gold; And my revenue than choice silver. I walk in the way of righteousness, In the midst of the paths of justice; That I may cause those that love me to inherit substance, And that I may fill their treasuries. [Jehovah possessed me in the beginning of his way, Before his works of old.* **I was set up from everlasting, from the beginning, Before the earth was.** *When there were no depths, I was brought forth, When there were no fountains abounding with water. Before the mountains were settled, Before the hills was I brought forth; While as yet he had not made the earth, nor the fields, Nor the beginning of the dust of the world.* **When he established the heavens, I was there**: *When he set a circle upon the face of the deep, When he made firm the skies above, When the fountains of the deep became strong, When he gave to the sea its bound, That the waters should not transgress his commandment, When he marked out the foundations of the earth;* **Then I was by him, as a master workman**; *And I was daily his delight, Rejoicing always before him, Rejoicing in his habitable earth; And my delight was with the sons of men. Now therefore, my sons, hearken*

A Conversation with Wisdom

unto me; For blessed are they that keep my ways. Hear instruction, and be wise, And refuse it not. Blessed is the man that heareth me, Watching daily at my gates, Waiting at the posts of my doors. **For whoso findeth me findeth life, And shall obtain favor of Jehovah.** *But he that sinneth against me wrongeth his own soul: All they that hate me love death.] (Pro. 8:3-36, ASV)*

All true wisdom springs from God-and it is evident in His handiwork. It is an uncreated, interminable wisdom that existed before anything or anyone else was. It is creative, prudent, masterful, and skillful. We can trust God's wisdom because He knows the best course of action in every possible scenario a human being may face. There is a right way and a wrong way to live-to speak, act, think, handle money, interact with others, and manage one's emotions. There are wise and foolish ways to govern, pursue wealth, and enter into covenants with others. If we embrace wisdom, the favor and blessing of the Lord will follow. By contrast, no good can come from spurning His instruction. Even if the wicked seem to prosper, in the end they will be cut off (Ps. 73).

2.3.1   EXERCISE

Write a brief response to this passage, focusing on verses 3-21. What is prudence (v. 5, 12)? What is the fear of the Lord, according to this passage? What is durable wealth?

2.3.2   EXERCISE

Find the references that pertain to each statement:
a) Wisdom comes from God Himself. Prov. _____
b) Wisdom existed from the beginning. Prov. ____

A Conversation with Wisdom

What are some "excellent things" spoken by wisdom in Prov. 8:6?

How do you see "truth" in Prov. 8:7? What is an abomination? What does it mean to be "crooked" or "perverse?"

Is loving righteousness the same as hating wickedness? Why or why not?

2.4 WISDOM-THIRD SPEECH

Wisdom hath builded her house; She hath hewn out her seven pillars: She hath killed her beasts; She hath mingled her wine; She hath also furnished her table: She hath sent forth her maidens; She crieth upon the highest places of the city: Whoso is simple, let him turn in hither: As for him that is void of understanding, she saith to him, Come, eat ye of my bread, And drink of the wine which I have mingled. Leave off, ye simple ones, and live; And walk in the way of understanding. He that correcteth a scoffer getteth to himself reviling; And he that reproveth a wicked man getteth himself a blot. Reprove not a scoffer, lest he hate thee: Reprove a wise man, and he will love thee. **Give instruction to a wise man, and he will be yet wiser: Teach a righteous man, and he will increase in learning**. *The fear of Jehovah is the beginning of wisdom; And the knowledge of the Holy One is understanding.* **For by me thy days shall be multiplied, And the years of thy life shall be increased**. *If thou art wise, thou art wise for thyself; And if thou scoffest, thou alone shalt bear it. (Proverbs 9:1-12)*

A Conversation with Wisdom

Wisdom literally invites people to share in her benefits. There is no excuse for failing to heed her calls-and as we walk in the Spirit and digest the Word of God, the fruit of godly wisdom should show in our lives. Furthermore, wise Christian leaders are a blessing-and if we respond appropriately to their correction or reproof, we will love them for their honesty and not become bitter. They warn us so that we can advance in our process of becoming more like Christ. True ministers are interested in our preparation, edification and maturation (Col. 1:28; Eph. 4:11-13).

Just as wisdom cries aloud in the streets, inviting whosoever will to come in and gain understanding, so the preachers of the gospel are everywhere, blanketing the streets with the message of salvation by grace through faith in Jesus' atoning work. The wisest decision that can ever be made is to repent and believe the gospel, accepting Jesus as Savior and Lord. To refuse Him is to embrace death-and the one who does this is harming himself forever. We are all responsible for the choices we make in life. Those who are wise, are wise for themselves; those who scoff (make mockery) will suffer the repercussions alone.

2.4.1   EXERCISE

Have you ever tried to correct a scoffer or a wicked person? Have you ever had to reprove a wise person? If so, what was the result of that encounter? Write a short response to this speech, and include a note about your experience. Identify three benefits of wisdom mentioned in this passage.

2.5 FOLLY ALSO SPEAKS - BUT DON'T LISTEN!

The foolish woman is clamorous; She is simple, and knoweth nothing. And she sitteth at the door of her house, On a seat in the high places of the city, To call to them that pass by, Who go right on their ways: Whoso is simple, let him turn in *hither; **And as for him that is void of understanding, she saith to him, Stolen waters are sweet, And bread eaten in secret is pleasant**. But he knoweth not that the dead are there; That her guests are in the depths of Sheol. (Proverbs 9:13-18)*

Folly calls out to pedestrians also, inviting them to embrace her unseemly ways. Where Wisdom has prepared a lavish, full-course banquet for her guests, complete with instruction and insight, Folly offers only bread and water, enjoyed the shadows where it is presumed no one else will see. Folly preys on the credulous and the unwary-those who have refused the call to wisdom. Her entreaties are based on "the lust of the eye, the lust of the flesh, and the pride of life" (1 Jn. 2:16). She savors unrighteous motives and the thought of "getting away with it." As a counterfeit to wisdom, Folly pretends to offer things of lasting value, but the pleasures of sin only last for a season (Heb. 11:25).

When Folly calls, refuse to listen! That is the time to engage in spiritual warfare because you have encountered a proposition that exalts itself against the knowledge of God (2 Cor. 10:5). Choose wisdom. Choose life. Choose the fear of the Lord!

2.5.1 EXERCISE

What does this mean to you? Write about a time in life when Folly called out to you and you refused to listen. If you did listen, write about the consequences of engaging in something unwise, and what you learned from it.

2.6 THE WORDS OF THE ADULTERESS

And I beheld among the simple ones, I discerned among the youths, A young man void of understanding, Passing through the street near

A Conversation with Wisdom

her corner; And he went the way to her house, In the twilight, in the evening of the day, In the middle of the night and in the darkness. And, behold, there met him a woman With the attire of a harlot, and wily of heart. She is clamorous and willful; Her feet abide not in her house: Now she is in the streets, now in the broad places, And lieth in wait at every corner. So she caught him, and kissed him, And with an impudent face she said unto him: Sacrifices of peace-offerings are with me; This day have I paid my vows. Therefore came I forth to meet thee, Diligently to seek thy face, and I have found thee. I have spread my couch with carpets of tapestry, With striped cloths of the yarn of Egypt. I have perfumed my bed With myrrh, aloes, and cinnamon. Come, let us take our fill of love until the morning; Let us solace ourselves with loves. For the man is not at home; He is gone a long journey: He hath taken a bag of money with him; He will come home at the full moon. With her much fair speech she causeth him to yield; With the flattering of her lips she forceth him along. He goeth after her straightway, As an ox goeth to the slaughter, Or as one in fetters to the correction of the fool; Till an arrow strike through his liver; As a bird hasteth to the snare, And knoweth not that it is for his life. (Proverbs 7:7-23)

These words come in the context of a father admonishing a son. It is the tale of a young man who lacked understanding-who ends up caught in the snare of an adulterous woman (Pro. 6:32). Not only does he become an object of reproach and dishonor, but he also becomes the target of her husband's wrath. He cannot make up for the wrong he has done by restoring what was taken away (Pro. 6:34-35).

A Conversation with Wisdom

Paul tells us that one who sins sexually sins against his own body (1 Cor. 6:18).

Notice how this woman appeals to the lust of the flesh, and encourages him in the way of deceit and secret indulgence. She is the opposite of the Virtuous Woman, whom we will consider in the next section. The young man in this illustration succumbs to temptation, but God makes a way of escape for every temptation that we face (1 Cor. 10:13). Furthermore, the apostle James tells us not to blame God for our temptations, because He does not tempt us. Instead, "every man is tempted, when he is drawn away of his own lust, and enticed" (Jas. 1:13-14).

2.6.1   EXERCISE

Write a brief response to this passage. Why is this young man compared to an ox headed for slaughter? What can we learn from this passage about being in the wrong place at the wrong time?

2.7 VIRTUOUS WOMAN- SPEECH

A worthy woman who can find? For her price is far above rubies. The heart of her husband trusteth in her, And he shall have no lack of gain. She doeth him good and not evil All the days of her life. She seeketh wool and flax, And worketh willingly with her hands. She is like the merchant-ships; She bringeth her bread from afar. She riseth also while it is yet night, And giveth food to her household, And their task to her maidens. She considereth a field, and buyeth it; With the fruit of her hands she planteth a vineyard. She girdeth her loins with strength, And maketh strong her arms. She perceiveth that her merchandise is profitable: Her lamp

A Conversation with Wisdom

goeth not out by night. She layeth her hands to the distaff, And her hands hold the spindle. She stretcheth out her hand to the poor; Yea, she reacheth forth her hands to the needy. She is not afraid of the snow for her household; For all her household are clothed with scarlet. She maketh for herself carpets of tapestry; Her clothing is fine linen and purple. Her husband is known in the gates, When he sitteth among the elders of the land. She maketh linen garments and selleth them, And delivereth girdles unto the merchant. Strength and dignity are her clothing; And she laugheth at the time to come. She openeth her mouth with wisdom; And the law of kindness is on her tongue. She looketh well to the ways of her household, And eateth not the bread of idleness. Her children rise up, and call her blessed; Her husband also, and he praiseth her, saying: Many daughters have done worthily, But thou excellest them all. Grace is deceitful, and beauty is vain; But a woman that feareth Jehovah, she shall be praised. Give her of the fruit of her hands; And let her works praise her in the gates. (Proverbs 31:10-31)

Women figure prominently in the book of Proverbs. In many ways, this chapter is the crown jewel of the book. Last to be read, this famous poem describing the Virtuous Woman shows us what wisdom looks like when applied in a life; both practically and spiritually. She is governed by reverence for the Lord, and this leads her to manage her time, money words, and talents in ways fully consistent with divine wisdom. Her priorities are in order. A wise woman lives a balanced life in which God is first. She cares for her family, community and career, but does not neglect herself in the process.

2.8 NOTABLE LESSONS FOR WOMEN FROM THE BOOK OF PROVERBS

- ✓ Avoid street life (Pro. 7:10-12)
- ✓ Avoid gossip (Pro. 11:13)
- ✓ Do not harbor anger/associate with those given to anger (Pro. 16:32; 19:11; and 22:24-25)
- ✓ Don't be contentious (Pro. 21:19; 27:15)
- ✓ Don't bring shame to your spouse (Pro. 12:4)
- ✓ Don't work toward the destruction of your own house (Pro. 14:1)
- ✓ Refuse to be lazy or an underachiever (Pro. 31:15, 27)
- ✓ Dress well, but know that true beauty lies within (Pro. 11:22; 31:22, 30)
- ✓ Dress your children well (Pro. 31:21)
- ✓ Discipline your children (Pro. 23:13-14; 29:15)
- ✓ Train your children according to their "bent" (Pro. 22:6)
- ✓ Live so that your children will bless you later (Pro. 31:28)
- ✓ Speak kindly to others (Pro. 31:26)
- ✓ Have your own business (Pro. 31:24)
- ✓ Make investments (Pro. 31:16)
- ✓ Be faithful to your vows (Pro. 31:11-12)
- ✓ Bring delight/pleasure to your spouse (Pro. 5:18-19)
- ✓ Develop your skills (Pro. 31: 13, 19)
- ✓ Manage others (Pro. 31:15)
- ✓ Know how to cook/ know how to travel for a bargain (Pro. 31:14-15)
- ✓ Know how to decorate your home to create an atmosphere (Pro. 24:3-4)
- ✓ Be compassionate, charitable toward others (Pro. 31:20)
- ✓ Fear the Lord (Pro. 31:30-31)

A Conversation with Wisdom

Pray for these characteristics to be developed in your life. Pray instead of living in anxiety and fear about your shortcomings and failures, because you will never be dynamic until you become specific about what you need the Lord to do in your life. What is it today? Is it developing a charitable heart? Is it speaking life to your family instead of negativity? Or is it going back to school, starting that business, or investing that money instead of spending it on a new outfit? At every turn, there are opportunities to put the wisdom of God's word into practice-and experience the blessing that comes from so doing. Christian men should also study these passages-they will be helpful to singles in seeking out the right kind of help meet.

[Teacher's Notes: 1) Many theologians note that the discussion in Proverbs 8:22-36 shifts from Wisdom in the poetic sense to the eternal Son of God, as indicated by the words "I was beside Him as one brought up," and other implicit declarations of His preexistence. The thought is that as wisdom has always existed, so He has always existed, and that if you find Wisdom/find Him, you will have life (compare Pro.8:35 with John 17:3). Advanced students will be interested in studying how this passage relates to the nature and composition of the Godhead (the historical debate between Trinitarian thought and Sabellianism/Modalism). Paul goes into detail about God's wisdom and power in 1 Corinthians 1:17, but this will lead away from the focus on practical application and leans more toward hermeneutics and exegesis; 2) Challenge the women in the class to examine this list closely and pray about those areas which need improvement; and 3) To bring this lesson forward in to the New Testament, point students to Jesus' parable of the Wise and Foolish Virgins or the parable of the Wise and Foolish Builders (Matt. 7:26; Matt 25:2).]

A Conversation with Wisdom

A Conversation with Wisdom

For we also once were foolish, disobedient, deceived, serving divers lusts and pleasures, living in malice and envy, hateful, hating one another. But when the kindness of God our Saviour, and his love toward man, appeared...
Paul the Apostle

CHAPTER THREE

FOUR TYPES OF FOOLS

In this chapter we will take a closer look at the character of the fool. When the Bible talks about a "fool," it does not just indicate a stupid or slow person, although that is certainly included. Instead, it highlights an attitude of self-sufficiency, self-confident boasting, and rebellion against established order-in short, arrogance. A fool, then, is someone whose lifestyle is orchestrated as if there were no God. This is the lie he tells himself in his heart (Ps. 53:1). Fools can be broken down into four categories. They are:

- ✓ THE SIMPLE FOOL
- ✓ THE ARROGANT FOOL
- ✓ THE SCOFFER
- ✓ THE REBEL

3.1 THE SIMPLE FOOL

This type of person is unable to discern between truth and falsehood, because they lack direction and are headed for a fall. They love simplicity, and delight in mockery. This means that they refuse to attain understanding, particularly as it relates to divine principles, and that knowledge is hated or "utterly odious" to them.

How long, ye simple ones, will ye love simplicity? And scoffers delight them in scoffing, And fools hate knowledge? (Pro. 1:22 ASV)

The simple fool is void of understanding. This scripture is found within a poignant story about the dangers of youthful lust, and "simple" here carries the meaning of being "seducible."

And I beheld among the simple ones, I discerned among the youths, A young man void of understanding... (Pro. 7:7)

As discussed in the previous chapter, this young man was walking along the road, likely in a place where he should never have been, when a woman dressed like a harlot approached him. She led him (or he allowed himself to be led) into illicit relations with her, trusting that "the man is not at home. He is on a long journey." (Pro. 7:19) This act of foolish indulgence cost him his life-

"Till an arrow strike through his liver; As a bird hasteth to the snare, And knoweth not that it is for his life." (Pro. 7:23)

This young man did not use wisdom. He did not weigh the consequences of his actions. He also trusted someone whom he had no reason to trust. However, the worst failure on

A Conversation with Wisdom

his part was that he did not demonstrate the fear of the LORD in the midst of temptation. Observe Joseph's response to the same temptation:

> *And it came to pass after these things, that his master's wife cast her eyes upon Joseph; and she said, Lie with me. But he refused, and said unto his master's wife, Behold, my master knoweth not what is with me in the house, and he hath put all that he hath into my hand: he is not greater in this house than I; neither hath he kept back anything from me but thee, because thou art his wife: how then can I do this great wickedness, and sin against God? And it came to pass, as she spake to Joseph day by day, that he hearkened not unto her, to lie by her, or to be with her. (Genesis 39:7-10)*

Both of these men were young, and subject to the same kind of temptation (the lust of the flesh), but the first moved in folly and plunged right in to his own detriment, whereas the fear of the LORD moved Joseph to behave wisely. Youth is not an excuse for plunging in to ruin-many times there is a failure to weigh the situation wisely (count the cost), or to take the LORD into account when making difficult decisions.

The simple fool is gullible and tends to fall into deception. He refuses to acquire critical knowledge and make sound choices based on truth.

> *The foolish woman is clamorous; She is simple, and knoweth nothing. (Pro. 9:13)*

In this context from which this verse is taken, Wisdom and Folly are presented as two women, who are offering invitations to those who pass by. Wisdom aims to save and enrich those who take heed-she reminds them to fear the LORD. The foolish woman speaks delusions to entice the unsuspecting, saying "Stolen waters are sweet, and bread eaten in secret is pleasant" (Pro. 9:17). See also 2 Tim. 3:1-6.

God has given mankind fair warning-indulgence in folly leads to death. The foolish will die for rejecting wisdom. Backsliding and careless ease are serious causes for concern. If there is no turning point; no "coming to oneself" in repentance; and no seeking of wisdom in humility and faith, then the end result is clear.

> *For the backsliding of the simple shall slay them, And the careless ease of fools shall destroy them. (Pro. 1:32 ASV)*

Sadly, folly begets more folly (Pro. 3:35; 14:18, 24). However, in the miracle of regeneration, we are able to ask the Lord for wisdom. The believer does not have to make unwise choices! The anointing of the Holy Ghost cancels the destructive cycle so that we don't pass these choices or their consequences on to our children (Isa. 10:27).

FIVE TRAITS OF SIMPLE FOOLS

- ✓ They love simplicity (Pro. 1:22)
- ✓ They are devoid of understanding (Pro. 7:7)
- ✓ They are gullible (Pro. 9:13)
- ✓ They will die for turning away from wisdom (Pro. 1:32)
- ✓ They are destined for folly (Pro. 14:18, 24)

3.1.1 EXERCISE

Write about the mercy of God in turning a fool away from his folly and bringing his heart to a place of wisdom and communion with Him. In what ways have your experiences with the Lord made you wiser to the plots and schemes of the enemy to thwart your destiny in God?

3.1.2 EXERCISE

Write about the snare of gullibility and how these passages can help you to guard against it.

3.2 THE SCOFFER

The word "scoffer" is used to describe a person who mocks, derides or makes fun of something. This type of person laughs at wisdom and toys with wickedness. When warned of the consequences they say, "it won't happen to me." Another word for "scoffer" is "mocker," or someone who laughs at, puts down or scorns serious things or matters that they do not understand, to their own shame and detriment. It also carries with it the thought of making a mockery of something by way of imitation or interpretation. The Hebrew word has been translated "buffoon," whereas the Greek word implies a "derider" or "false teacher." We have an indication of the spirit of a scoffer in Peter's second epistle:

Knowing this first, that in the last days mockers shall come with mockery, walking after their own lusts, and saying, Where is the promise of his coming? for, from the day that the fathers fell asleep, all things continue as they were from the beginning of the creation. For this they willfully forget, that there were heavens from of old, and an earth compacted out of water and amidst water, by the word of God; by which means the world that then was, being overflowed with water, perished: (2Pe 3:3-6 ASV)

Throughout the scriptures, there have always been those who scoffed at God's word and His people, always to their own detriment. In terms of eschatology, there have been scoffers in every age since the Church began, who reject the truth of Jesus' second coming. A scoffing spirit is rooted in natural, human wisdom, which is incapable of discovering the true wisdom inspired by the Spirit (1 Cor. 2:13-14).

A Conversation with Wisdom

NOTABLE SCOFFERS

- ✓ Scoffers during the crucifixion (Mat. 27:29)
- ✓ Ishmael scoffed at Isaac (Gen. 21:9-10)
- ✓ Shimei scoffed at David (2 Sa. 16:5-11)
- ✓ Scoffers in the end times (2 Pet. 3:3)
- ✓

SIX TRAITS OF SCOFFERS

- ✓ They shame those who try to correct them (Pro. 9:7-8, 15:12)
- ✓ They refuse to listen to a rebuke (Pro. 13:1)
- ✓ They search for wisdom on their own in vain (Pro. 14:6)
- ✓ They cause contention and strife (Pro. 22:10A)
- ✓ They receive God's scorn (Pro. 3:34)
- ✓ They will inevitably face judgment (Pro. 19:29)

3.2.1 EXERCISE

Search the Scriptures. Find an example of someone who refused to listen to rebuke and suffered for it. Find an example of someone who embraced correction and responded to it correctly, ultimately becoming wiser for it. Prepare to discuss.

3.2.2 EXERCISE

Explain how we should respond to those who scoff at the claims of the gospel. Then explain how you might guard against a scoffing attitude in your own life. Consider what might happen in the natural realm if we scoff at a doctor's advice and continue to consume unhealthy foods.

3.3 THE ARROGANT FOOL

This kind of fool willfully ignores wisdom and lives only for himself. He has no interest in whether something is good or evil. His only question is "what's in it for me?" An arrogant fool will always have a justified hustle. Among other things, they despise authority, are a danger to others and to themselves, and are perfectly wise in their own opinion. Perhaps these were the kinds of people who lived during the days of the judges. It was said that "every man did what was right in his own eyes" and as you might expect, disaster was the result (Jdg. 21:25).

Arrogance, or pride, is a thing particularly detestable to God (Pro. 8:13). Although we may think of a man with his chest stuck out and head held high in overplayed self-confidence, pride can manifest itself in quiet, smug, or sly ways as well. Such persons will not heed wisdom - they do not feel they need it, and will not humble themselves in any case. We are warned not to boast in the wisdom of man. Humility places your soul in position to receive wisdom from the Lord.

> *Let no man deceive himself. If any man thinketh that he is wise among you in this world, let him become a fool, that he may become wise. For the wisdom of this world is foolishness with God. (1Co 3:18-19a ASV)*

NOTABLE ARROGANT FOOLS:

- ✓ Nabal (1 Sam. 25:1-39)
- ✓ Herod (Acts 12:21-23)
- ✓ Parable: man building bigger barns (Lk. 12:16-21)
- ✓ Sennacherib/ Rab-shakeh (2 Ki. 19:19; 19:16)

SIX TRAITS OF ARROGANT FOOLS

- ✓ They make sport out of doing evil (Pro. 10:23

- ✓ They rage at instruction (Pro. 14:16)
- ✓ They despise parents (Pro. 15:20)
- ✓ They are more dangerous than they think (Pro. 17:12)
- ✓ They prefer to give opinion rather than learn (Pro. 18:2)
- ✓ They are wise in their own eyes (Pro. 26:5)

3.3.1 EXERCISE

Read James (Jas. 4:6-10). What is the biblical remedy for an arrogant attitude? Why is boasting and self-seeking incompatible with wisdom? What is the root of this attitude?

3.4 THE REBEL

Rebellion is the underlying component of all foolishness. This rebellion can be in word, thought, or deed. Remember that even "the thought of foolishness is sin." (Pro. 24:9) A rebel is a person who is argumentative and walks in constant opposition to rules and order. He actually hates wisdom and is an aggressive unbeliever. Rebels are headed on the path toward destruction.

King Saul was instructed to execute the Amalekites, not sparing anyone and not partaking of the spoil. Instead, persuaded by the demands of the people, he preserved the life of King Agag and kept the best of the sheep and oxen to be used as offerings to the Lord (1 Sa. 15:8-9). Saul made excuses and concessions, but the verdict of God had been rendered:

> ...Hath Jehovah as great delight in burnt-offerings and sacrifices, as in obeying the voice of Jehovah? Behold, to obey is better than sacrifice, and to hearken than the fat of rams. For rebellion is as the sin of witchcraft, and stubbornness is as iniquity and idolatry.

Because thou hast rejected the word of Jehovah, he hath also rejected thee from being king. (1Sa 15:22-23 ASV)

The application here is that partial obedience is still disobedience.

NOTABLE REBELS

- ✓ Absalom (2 Sa. 15:1-13)
- ✓ Korah, Dathan, and Abiram (Num. 16-1-14)
- ✓ Vashti, Queen of Persia (Est. 1:12-16)
- ✓ Children of Israel (Ezek. 20:21)
- ✓ Saul of Tarsus (Acts 26:14)

NINE TRAITS OF REBELS

- ✓ They despise wisdom (Pro. 1:7)
- ✓ They are sure they are right (Pro. 12:15)
- ✓ They mock the idea of sin (Pro. 14:9)
- ✓ They despise parents instruction (Pro. 15:5)
- ✓ They try self correction (Pro. 16:22)
- ✓ They argue easily (Pro. 20:3)
- ✓ They cannot be separated from foolishness (Pro. 27:22)
- ✓ They are destined for a fall (Pro. 10:8)
- ✓ They will die for lack of wisdom (Pro. 10:21)

3.4.1 EXERCISE

Explain how the graces of humility and submission can guard us from a rebellious attitude. In keeping with Jesus' teaching in Mat. 5:22, why is it wrong to call people "worthless" or "fool" (lit. "blockhead")?

3.4.2　　EXERCISE

After breaking up into small groups, come up with a 3-5 minute skit that illustrates the behavior of one type of fool. Focus on poor choices and their consequences. Each skit must also illustrate the path of wisdom taken in the same situation. Make the connection between the lesson and how we should govern ourselves as Christians walking wisely in today's world.

THE KINGDOM KIND OF FOOL

In the New Testament, there is one kind of fool that it's good to be called, and that's a "fool for Christ's sake." This means that the believer is actively bearing the reproach of the cross and the mockery of the world. The apostles were called fools by the world because of the suffering they endured to preach the gospel to those in need (Acts 26:24; 1 Cor. 4:9-10). What a privilege to be reviled for the name of Christ!

[Teacher's Notes: 1) Pull out examples of each kind of fool or from ancient or modern history. Also, discuss the first incidence of pride as it relates to the devil (Ezek. 28:12-17). A thorough review of his "I will" statements and subsequent eviction from heaven should accentuate this lesson for more advanced students (Isa. 14:12-15); 2) Explain in detail the reasons for God's command regarding the Amalekites, and the fruit of his actions which did not appear until hundreds of years later during the reign of Esther (1 Sam. 15:33; Est. 3:1; 7:6; and 9:14); 3) Address the state of man before regeneration and how that rebellion is brought to an end in Christ, using the conversion of Saul (Paul) as a starting point (Acts 9:1-18); and 4) Explain why, although we may recognize folly in others, we are not to refer to others as "fools" in a derogatory manner (Pro. 10:18; Mat. 5:22).]

A Conversation with Wisdom

Say not thou, What is the cause that the former days were better than these? For thou dost not inquire wisely concerning this.
King Solomon

CHAPTER FOUR

CHOOSING WHAT'S BETTER

An old expression by the French philosopher Voltaire (1694-1778) states that "the better is the enemy of the good." Making the best choice is not always easy. Our lives are equivalent to the sum of our choices. These choices can have serious implications as we seek to apprehend that for which we have been apprehended by Christ (Phil. 3:12).

We are often pressed to decide between good and evil- whether to yield to sin or persevere in holiness. At other times, we may have to settle on something positive, such as which college to attend or whether to pursue an employment opportunity. In moments of uncertainty, we are to yield to the Holy Ghost, waiting patiently as He guides us into the details of His will.

A Conversation with Wisdom

In this chapter, we will examine seven "better than" contrasts. They portray an important difference of perspective-because what the world may see as superior, the Lord may see as inferior; or what the world may consider to be of little value, God may declare that we cannot live without. The verses provide broad principles rather than specific commands, making them applicable to a multiplicity of issues.

4.1 WISDOM IS BETTER THAN WEALTH

*Happy is the man that findeth wisdom, and the man that getteth understanding. For the gaining of it is **better than** the gaining of silver, and the profit thereof than fine gold. (Pro. 3:13-14 ASV)*

She is more precious than rubies: And none of the things thou canst desire are to be compared unto her. (Pro. 8:11 ASV)

Wisdom is always better than wealth. However, this must not be seen as an excuse to remain poor (or to continue with an impoverished mentality). It simply means that wisdom is more profitable than mere money or material.

This scripture likens wisdom to commodities that pay proceeds to the one who possesses them. Those proceeds are better than anything one can find on the market for the price of silver; and its income or revenue is worth more than refined gold. Therefore, the man or woman who acquires wisdom and secures understanding (intelligence, discretion, or reason) is abundantly blessed. Further, nothing that a human being may desire on this side of heaven can truly be compared to wisdom. Proverbs 31 refers to the Virtuous Woman as a person whose value is far above rubies, and no wonder, for one of her chief characteristics is wisdom-the fear of the Lord!

It is possible for a person to be wealthy, yet fail to use their resources for righteous purposes. He may put confidence

A Conversation with Wisdom

in those riches or squander it foolishly. The Prodigal Son is a good example of this.

> *And he said, a certain man had two sons: and the younger of them said to his father, Father, give me the portion of thy substance that falleth to me. And he divided unto them his living. And not many days after, the younger son gathered all together and took his journey into a far country; and there he wasted his substance with riotous living. And when he had spent all, there arose a mighty famine in that country; and he began to be in want. (Luke 15:11 ASV)*

Conversely, a poor man with wisdom may lack the respect and privilege that accompanies wealth but yet be able to usher in great deliverance. Unfortunately, his words may be despised by those who consider themselves more mighty and powerful. King Solomon spoke of this in Ecclesiastes.

> *Now there was found in it a poor wise man, and he by his wisdom delivered the city; yet no man remembered that same poor man. Then said I, Wisdom [is]* **better than** *strength: nevertheless the poor man's wisdom [is] despised, and his words are not heard. (Eccl. 9: 16-17 KJV)*

The ultimate example of this is the Lord Jesus during His earthly ministry. His lowliness of life worked in perfect balance with His magnificent wisdom.

4.1.1   EXERCISE

Read Pro. 3:13-18. Identify five or more characteristics or possessions of wisdom within the passage.

4.2 LITTLE WITH THE FEAR OF THE LORD IS BETTER THAN GREAT RICHES ASSOCIATED WITH TROUBLE

> **Better** *is little, with the fear of Jehovah,* **than** *great treasure and trouble therewith. (Pro. 15:16)*

Wealth can be obtained by positive or negative means. Great riches can come from sinful activities such as fraud, bribery, illegal forms of business, gambling, and even overworking for the purpose of being rich. When a person fears the Lord, he or she will also hate evil, and decline to engage in activities that yield wealth through unrighteous means. How many times have we heard stories about riches that came with "trouble" attached? The fear of the Lord is better because it leads a person to depart from evil.

Similarly, remember that "a good name is rather to be chosen than great riches" (Pro. 22:1). A person may be wealthy, but if his name loses respectability, it will be very difficult for him to have a positive effect on others. Integrity is an attribute of those who walk uprightly. It is better, from God's perspective, to have less and maintain a good name, than to have material abundance with a bad reputation and poor character.

The word "trouble" in the Hebrew is *mehumah,* and indicates confusion or uproar, destruction, discomfiture, tumult or vexation. A righteous man may have less, but will experience peace while walking in the fear of the Lord. He will not be confused, headed for destruction or overly vexed. All of the money in the world, on the other hand, could not buy the blessedness that comes from depending on the Lord.

A Conversation with Wisdom

4.2.1 EXERCISE

Commit Pro. 15:16 to memory. Rephrase this proverb in your own words.

4.3 A SIMPLE MEAL WITH LOVE IS BETTER THAN A FEAST WITH HATRED

***Better** is a dinner of herbs, where love is, **than** a stalled ox and hatred therewith. (Pro. 15:17)*

There was a time when families sat down to dinner around the table and talked with each other about the events of their day. Times have changed, and very often this type of gathering is reserved for holidays, birthdays, and other special occasions. Still, we understand that it's the company and fellowship of the people at the table-not just what's *on* the table-that makes those occasions memorable. Mealtime is about fellowship.

No wonder the Word of God declares that a simple vegetarian meal, with love (i.e., family unity, brotherly fellowship, friendship, an honest business relationship), is to be preferred to a meat-filled, full course dining wonder where those at the table hate each other. The hatred could be hidden, or openly acknowledged. In that environment, who can really enjoy themselves? Heed this word:

Eat thou not the bread of him that hath an evil eye, Neither desire thou his dainties: For as he thinketh within himself, so is he: Eat and drink, saith he to thee; But his heart is not with thee. The morsel which thou hast eaten shalt thou vomit up, And lose thy sweet words. (Pro 23: 6-8 ASV)

4.3.1 EXERCISE

Commit Pro. 15:17 to memory. What does this scripture mean to you?

4.4 MAN WITH SELF CONTROL BETTER THAN HE WHO RULES A CITY

> *He that is slow to anger is **better than** the mighty; and he that ruleth his spirit, than he that taketh a city. (Pro. 16:32)*

The mighty man is able to conquer a city by exerting all of his natural power against his opponents and bringing them into subjection to his authority. History celebrates such men - renowned warriors such as Napoleon Bonaparte or Genghis Khan. Consider Joshua at the Battle of Ai or David when he recovered all from the Philistines (Josh. 8:1-28; 1 Sam. 30:17-20). Yet better than all of these is the man who is slow to anger and able to exercise self control. He has learned not to give into the heat of his emotions, and instead pauses to think through a situation. He *responds* to crisis-he does not *react*. (In 1 Sam. 25 Abigail stopped David from executing all of the males in her household in the heat of his rage.)

A man who controls his anger knows the danger of acting rashly and holds his peace. It is more challenging to bring yourself into alignment with the principles of God's kingdom than it is to subdue others! Paul spoke of beating his body to keep it into subjection (1 Cor. 9 27). The Holy Ghost produces the fruit of self-control (Gal. 5:22-23). Additionally, in order for men to be free in prayer and worship, their hands must be free of wrath (1 Ti. 2:8).

> *He whose spirit is without restraint is like a city that is broken down and without walls. (Pro.*

25:28 ASV)

This means that anything the enemy sends to invade your spirit can march into your life unhindered because you have not learned how to take control over your emotional life. This state of being contributes to psychological warfare and requires a deliberate suiting up in the armor of God and the deployment of spiritual weapons: namely, the Word, the Name of Jesus, and the Blood of Jesus.*

4.4.1 EXERCISE

Commit Pro. 16:32 to memory. With this principle in mind, write about why some young people are so angry today. Complete this statement: "Controlling my temper means I must..."

4.5 HUMBLE ASSOCIATIONS ARE BETTER THAN INCREASED RICHES WITH THE PROUD

Better *it is to be of a lowly spirit with the poor,* ***than*** *to divide the spoil with the proud. (Pro. 16:19 ASV)*

For 400 years the ancient Egyptians inflicted suffering on their Hebrew slaves, reaping the benefits of their hard labor. Moses, who would have been killed as part of mass infanticide, was spared, because God planned to use him to bring Israel out of bondage. Since Moses was raised in the palace as a prince of Egypt, it would have been easy for him to stay there, spending the increase produced by the Israelites' hard work. Instead, he chose to turn his back on the riches and power of Egypt in exchange for a shepherd's life (Heb. 11:24-26). He understood that the pleasure of sin was only temporary-not worth it for any amount of wealth or fame. If you are unsure of what matters most in life, weigh it in the light of eternity! (Eventually, the

A Conversation with Wisdom

Hebrew slaves plundered the Egyptians, taking that same wealth into the wilderness with them.)

4.5.1   EXERCISE

Commit Pro. 16:19 to memory. Why do you think this is true? Read the story of the Exodus (Ex. 14). Take a praise break.

4.6 BETTER TO HAVE LESS WITH HONESTY THAN A WITH CORRUPTION

> ***Better*** *is the poor that walketh in his integrity **than** he that is perverse in his lips and is a fool. Also, that the soul be without knowledge is not good; And he that hasteth with his feet sinneth. The foolishness of man subverteth his way; And his heart fretteth against Jehovah. (Pro. 19:1-3)*

> *Better is the poor that walketh in his integrity, than he that is perverse in his ways, though he be rich. (Pro. 28:6)*

> *It is better to be poor (have less) and honest than to be rich and crooked. A person may have less, but if he wakes in integrity (lit. "completeness" or "moral innocence"), he will enjoy a clear conscience knowing that he did not pursue dishonest gain. Integrity will be rewarded by the Lord, but folly will be punished. Remember that "a good name is rather to be chosen than riches" (Pro. 22:1). The mouth of the wicked person speaks perverse (lit. "distorted") things, broadcasting his folly.*

A Conversation with Wisdom

It is also foolish to be hasty. Decisions are meant to be prayed over and thought through - not rushed into without proper planning or preparation. Hastiness causes a man to sin or miss the right path. The timing of God is as important as the promises He makes.

There are those who act foolishly (lit. "impiously") and then blame God when their lives are ruined. This is extremely unwise! Instead of turning from sin and moving forward in righteousness, such people harbor anger toward God and cut off their own blessing. If a man refuses to work (while spending recklessly and living off of others), and consequences overtake him so that he is steeped in debt and his resources have dried up, he must not blame the Lord for his failure to obey the principles of wisdom. Before we get to the part where God flips the situation and brings him out into "a wealthy place," there must be repentance and humility toward God.

EXAMPLES OF MEN'S ANGER WITH GOD

CAIN. Cain brought an offering to God that was not solicited. He brought him the fruit of his own labor - and while he worked harder to produce it, it reflected a spirit of self-reliance, as opposed to Abel's offering, which pointed to reliance on the blood. Abel did not approach God with his best work - he approached God by faith through sacrifice. The Lord God told Cain exactly what to do: "Go and correct the problem. If you do the right thing, you will be rewarded. If not, sin is waiting for you - but it doesn't have to be this way." Cain's was angry - not only at Abel, out of jealousy, but ultimately at God for preferring Abel's sacrifice and rejecting his hard work. After all, he only wanted to please God. But is it not folly to bring to God what He does not want (Gen. 4:2-8)?

UZZAH. When the Ark of God was being returned to Israel from the land of the Philistines, David and all the people came out to celebrate. The Ark, which was meant to be carried with staves on the shoulders of the Levites, now sat on top of a filthy ox cart as it passed through the streets. When it began to topple, Uzzah put out his hand to keep it from falling and died. Why? They did not follow the Law with regard to its transport - and certainly, no unauthorized hand was to put their flesh to this powerful piece of tabernacle furniture. David, who knew better, was then angry with the Lord. After all, he only meant well. However, it was folly to treat the Ark of God as a common thing. God is holy! Later, his "displeasure" turned to fear (reverence), so that he distanced himself from the Ark. The next time he sought to bring the Ark of God back, he followed all of the instructions in the Law of Moses (2 Sa. 6:1-18).

4.6.1   EXERCISE

Commit Pro. 28:6 to memory. Do you think there is ever a good reason to be angry with God? Explain.

4.7 OPEN REBUKE IS BETTER THAN SECRET LOVE

> **Better** *is open rebuke **than** love that is hidden. Faithful are the wounds of a friend; But the kisses of an enemy are profuse. (Pro. 27:5-6)*
>
> *He that rebuketh a man shall afterward find more favor Than he that flattereth with the tongue. (Pro 28:23 ASV)*

It is more desirable to be reproved by a friend, whose love compels him not to leave us alone in our sins, than to be deeply loved by someone and yet never see that affection expressed beneficial ways (Jas. 5:20). The rebuke that comes by the mouth of a friend seems painful at first, but through honesty, he proves his faithfulness (Pro. 20:30). Note that even the loving confrontation of a friend or Christian brother/sister should be done prayerfully and delivered skillfully (Pro. 25:15;

A Conversation with Wisdom

Eph. 4:14). Consider the manner in which Nathan confronted David about his sin with Bathsheba (2 Sam. 12:1-7).

By contrast, the "kisses of an enemy are deceitful," and profuse displays of affection serve only as masks meant to cover their true evil intentions. Secret love does no good to anyone. God demonstrated His love toward us, and we should do likewise with one another (Rom. 5:8). Love will not flatter with its tongue, but speak the truth. We are called to "love not only in word, but in deed and truth" (1 Jn. 3:18).

Examples of open rebuke may be found in Paul's confrontation of Peter when he behaved hypocritically before the Jewish believers; and in the Corinthian church when a parishioner engaged in sexual relations with his stepmother (Gal. 2:11; 1 Cor. 5:1-3). Sinning elders are subject to public rebuke (1 Ti. 5:20). Judas remains the primary example of the betrayer's kiss (Luke 22:48). Love (or faith) that is not made manifest in deeds will speak blessing to the hungry and naked but not give him the things he needs (Jas. 2:16).

4.7.1   EXERCISE

Commit Pro. 27:5-6 to memory. Write about a time when you experienced the wound of a friend or the kiss of an enemy. How did you respond?

4.7.2   EXERCISE

Write a short paragraph on the difference between correction (which teaches us to do things the right way) and perfection (which aims to produce another level of maturity) in God's dealings with His people.

HINDRANCES TO CHOOSING WHAT IS BETTER
- ✓ Low-self-esteem
- ✓ Negative music/television and other vehicles of carnal entertainment

- ✓ Perverted (sexual) deadlocks
- ✓ Unwise associations/friendships
- ✓ Paralyzing fear/unbelief

4.8 CONCLUSION

The Book of Proverbs challenges us to use every resource at our disposal to navigate the choppy waters of this life. This means summoning information, intuition, conscience, love, patience, and truth in order to make the right choices. No matter how difficult it is, don't settle for a worldly, unsanctified lifestyle. Choose the fear of the Lord (Pro. 1:28-29). King Solomon, the man who had the best of anything the world can offer, said it this way:

> *And I turned myself to behold wisdom, and madness, and folly: for what can the man do that cometh after the king? even that which hath been done long ago. Then I saw that **wisdom excelleth folly, as far as light excelleth darkness**. (Eccl. 2:12-13 ASV)*

4.8.1　EXERCISE

Fill in the blanks. The first verse has been completed as an example. Rephrase each verse in your own words.

A Conversation with Wisdom

OTHER COMPARISONS

Reference	Better Is...	Than...
Pro 12:9	He that is lightly esteemed, and hath a servant	he that honoreth himself, and lacketh bread
Pro. 19:1		
Pro. 21:19		
Pro. 25:7		
Pro. 27:10		

[Teacher's Notes: 1) Emphasize to the class that although God is sovereign and works all things according to the counsel of His own will; He yet requires our obedience and holds us responsible for the choices we make. Through the Word of God and the Spirit of God, He gives us all the tools we need to make decisions that will glorify Him-to place a high premium not just on what is good, but what is better and best in this life; 2) Demonstrate that when they are faced with challenges in daily life, they can refer back to the principles of what is better, and so can know what to do. How should we live? Should we live in pursuit of the material at the expense of the prosperous soul? Discuss; 3) Pray with the class that they will make better life choices after this lesson and break the cycles that keep them from making true moral progress; 4) For students desiring deeper study, point them to the book of Hebrews for a discussion of the Better Covenant; Better Promises; Better

A Conversation with Wisdom

Hope; Better Resurrection, *et al.* See also Paul's desire to depart to be with Christ (which was better) versus remaining on earth which was needful (Phil. 1:23); 5) Caution against hastiness in spiritual and relational matters. One may be zealous to preach when they have not attained to spiritual maturity. Perhaps they are truly called to do this, but they have to be trained, prepared, and sent - not just by life experience, but also by diligent study of the Word of God. This takes time - with zeal there is a tendency to want everything "right now." Mention that marriage plans, relocations, and other major life decisions are also to be entered into with wise counsel, prayer and forethought; and 6) Explain the concept of psychological warfare.]

The highway of the upright is to depart from evil: He that keepeth his way preserveth his soul.
Proverbs 16:17

Control the controllable and avoid the avoidable.
Joseph N. Williams

CHAPTER FIVE

SETTING AND MAINTAINING WISE BOUNDARIES

This chapter examines the importance of setting and maintaining wise boundaries in daily life. Boundaries are hedges that fence you in to a place of safety and provision, ensuring that the dangers of the world remain at a distance. To disregard divinely ordained boundaries is to invite trouble. A wise person will set boundaries on his behavior so he routinely avoids evil, and associates with those who are "more redemptive than toxic." Boundaries also help to determine how much access others are given to speak into or over our lives.

A Conversation with Wisdom

5.1 PRUDENCE MEANS TAKING PRECAUTIONS

- ✓ Cautious Nature + Good Judgment (considering likely consequences and taking appropriate action) = Prudence

A prudent man seeth the evil, and hideth himself; But the simple pass on, and suffer for it. (Pro. 22:3)

Hiding oneself from impending danger also implies separation from evil associations, environments and influences that would attract God's displeasure. A prudent man perceives through foresight that the wicked will face punishment and seeks to hide himself from this by fleeing to God for help (Ps. 139:19, 23-24). Prayer releases the power to make wise choices! Those who are simple (foolish), do not take stock of God's warnings and suffer for their waywardness and disobedience to the truth (Pro. 15:4; 29:1).

5.1.1 EXERCISE

Memorize Pro. 22:3. How does removing yourself from evil associations and environments help your walk with God? How does it help physically, emotionally, and spiritually? In what ways can you limit bad influences or associations? Write two paragraphs about this.

5.2 BOUNDARIES & THE FATHER'S HEART

The heart of a father, like that of our Heavenly Father, sets boundaries in place for the good of his children. If a father tells his son not to play on the highway, but remain within the gates around their front yard, it is for a reason. He knows the dangers that threaten to cut down his son's life. Sometimes he

A Conversation with Wisdom

will explain the danger, at other times he might not. Obedience is the child's proper response to his instruction (Heb. 12:9).

When Paul wrote to the Corinthians on the matter of abstinence in singleness, he told them that he was not trying to lock them down in an unreasonable fashion, but was advising them as one who knew what was best for their lives (1 Cor. 7:35). Following his instructions would produce blessing, not bondage. Likewise, leaders in the Body of Christ remind of us of the boundaries God has placed on believers and apply discipline for transgressing them. Still, some boundaries are specific to the individual, because failing to keep them opens the door to a tailor-made temptation or demonic attack (Rom. 14:2-3; Jas. 1:14).

Youth are especially prone to transgressing the boundaries that are set for them (Pro. 22:15). Many passages in Proverbs are written as admonitions from a father to his son. Obedience on the part of the son/child produces joy in the heart of the father (Pro. 10:1).

WHERE OUR BOUNDARIES COME FROM:

- ✓ Conscience (Rom. 2:15)
- ✓ Reading Scripture (2 Tim. 3:16)
- ✓ Promptings of the Holy Ghost (Acts 8:29)
- ✓ Admonitions from spiritual leaders (Heb. 13:17)
- ✓ True prophetic utterances (Acts 11:28)
- ✓ The State/law (Rom. 13:3-4)
- ✓ Culture/Manner of Upbringing (Luke 18:20-21)
- ✓ Instructions of Parents (Pro. 13:1)
- ✓ Employer Institutions (Eph. 6:5-6, 9)
- ✓ Advice from Others (Pro. 12:15)

AREAS WHERE BOUNDARIES ARE OFTEN NEEDED

- ✓ How we spend money
- ✓ How we manage our emotions

- ✓ How we pursue relationships
- ✓ Where we spend our time
- ✓ Knowing when to say "no" to others (not allowing others to take unfair advantage)

5.3 TYPES OF BOUNDARIES

God surrounds His people with protective hedges, as He did with Job (1:8-12). However, there are times of intense testing and trial when He allows that hedge to be lifted, giving the enemy access to afflict/attack us. His goal in allowing this is our perfection, not our destruction! Job was blessed even more at the end of his life than he was before going through those tragic experiences. Paul said that the things he suffered actually worked out for the furtherance of the gospel (Phi. 1:12-14).

There is another sense in which the Father imposes boundaries on our lives that can't be crossed. An example of this would be when Moses wanted to enter Canaan but was forbidden to do so (Deut. 34:4). David wanted to build a house for God. While God did not allow him to do this, he enabled David to envision its design and lay up materials for use in that massive undertaking (2 Sam. 7:5, 12-13). Paul wanted to go to Asia on his missionary journey, but was forbidden by the Holy Ghost; however, he later received a vision to go to Macedonia, where his help was urgently needed (Acts 16:10-16). Our lives can be just like the waters of the sea, to which God said, "Thus far shall you progress, and no further" (Job 38:11).

5.4 KNOW YOUR LIMITS

Wisdom requires that we know ourselves well. If we are to live successful Christian lives, we must understand our particular blend of strengths and weaknesses. Knowing the things that attract our attention and threaten to interrupt our fellowship with God and each other, we can be better armed to pray through tests and temptations. We will know what things

A Conversation with Wisdom

to avoid, and what things need to be brought into subjection. Instead of trying to push boundary lines to their limits, we will be governed by the fear of the Lord, and say, "I think I should abstain from every *appearance* of evil," even if it is not necessarily forbidden.

Some saints struggle in areas so specific that in order to avoid falling into a trap (or walking into one with both eyes wide open), they must make special lifestyle adjustments. Whatever your temptation may be, you must avoid putting yourself in situations where you know it will be present. Never tell yourself you can handle it, because pride comes before a destruction and we are to place no confidence in the flesh (Pro. 16:18; Phil. 3:3). No, "let him who thinks he can stand take heed lest he fall" (1 Cor. 10:12).

The following are lists of some things the Bible warns us to avoid or control. It is not exhaustive, but will serve as a springboard for your prayer and consideration.

THINGS TO AVOID/SHUN:

- ✓ The pathway of the wicked (Pro. 4:14)
- ✓ Foolish questions about genealogies, strivings about the law (Tit. 3:9)
- ✓ Foolish and unlearned questions (2 Tim. 2:23)
- ✓ Profane and vain babblings (1 Tim. 6:20)
- ✓ Fornication, Adultery (1 Thess. 4:3)
- ✓ Youthful lusts (2 Tim. 2:22)
- ✓ Beholding base things with the eyes (Ps. 101:3)
- ✓ Those who cause divisions contrary to the gospel (Rom. 16:17)
- ✓ Unfruitful works of darkness (Eph. 3:11)
- ✓ Evil speaking/coarse jesting (Eph. 5:4)
- ✓ All appearance of evil (1 Thess 5:22)
- ✓ All falsehood (Ps. 119:104)
- ✓ Taking on the debts of others (Pro. 6:1-3)
- ✓ [Food offered to] idols, things strangled, blood (Acts 15:29)

- ✓ Fleshly lusts that war against the soul (1 Pet. 2:11)

THINGS TO BRING UNDER CONTROL
- ✓ Your physical body (1 Cor. 9:27)
- ✓ Your spirit (Pro. 25:28)
- ✓ Your thought life (Phil. 4:8)
- ✓ Your temper (Eccl. 7:9)
- ✓ Your tongue/words (Jas. 3:8-10)

5.4.1 EXERCISE

There are three areas in which we must know God's will and demonic set-ups. They are: 1) social pressure, 2) sexual pressure, and 3) emotional imbalance. Write about how one of these areas affects you. Find at least one scripture containing a warning about that area and memorize it. (Do not hand this in. It is for your reference.)

5.5 THE TRAP OF PHARISAISM

There is a danger in becoming Pharisaical with lifestyle boundaries. If we are not careful, we can make the principles that help govern our lives into hard and fast rules which everyone else must follow. They become works-based traditions that in turn become a false measure of holiness for an entire people. If something is not clearly expressed in Scripture, the individual must walk in a clear conscience before the Lord on the matter, and should not be judged by others about it. On the same note, that person must be mindful not to put a stumbling block in someone else's way. Consider the following Scriptures:

> *And there are gathered together unto him the Pharisees, and certain of the scribes, who had come from Jerusalem, and had seen that some of*

A Conversation with Wisdom

his disciples ate their bread with defiled, that is, unwashen, hands. (For the Pharisees, and all the Jews, except they wash their hands diligently, eat not, holding the tradition of the elders; and when they come from the market-place, except they bathe themselves, they eat not; and many other things there are, which they have received to hold, washings of cups, and pots, and brasen vessels.) And the Pharisees and the scribes ask him, Why walk not thy disciples according to the tradition of the elders, but eat their bread with defiled hands? (Mar 7:1-5 ASV)

If ye died with Christ from the rudiments of the world, why, as though living in the world, do ye subject yourselves to ordinances, Handle not, nor taste, nor touch (all which things are to perish with the using), after the precepts and doctrines of men? Which things have indeed a show of wisdom in will-worship, and humility, and severity to the body; but are not of any value against the indulgence of the flesh. (Col 2:20-23 ASV)

Ultimately, it comes down to the Spirit-filled, Spirit-led life. If we are filled with the Holy Ghost, we will not fulfill the desires of the carnal nature. The more we see our need of Him, the more we must cry out for His anointing to break every yoke. The more of Him we receive, the more of Him we want, and His transforming work will usher us to greater dimensions of glory. As we walk in the Spirit, we become occupied with expanding and experiencing the Kingdom-not with making new rules and resolutions for self-reform.

A Conversation with Wisdom

5.6 THE COMPANY YOU KEEP

The wise are mindful of the company they keep. They consider whether their associations are positive, edifying, and mutually beneficial; or negative, discouraging, and draining. A good friend may hit a rough patch and need some help getting back on his feet, which is understandable. But if he or she continues along a determined path of evil, that camaraderie has met an impasse - at least until a change of heart and behavior proves otherwise. This is because corruption is transferrable (Hag. 2:11-13). Paul explains this in his first letter to the Corinthians, a prescriptive epistle that corrected inappropriate behavior in the church (1 Cor. 5:9-13). A consecrated lifestyle calls for separation from those who persist in unholy living. Amos 3:3 asks: "Can two walk together except they be agreed?" We should avoid:

- ✓ **FORNICATORS** : those who practice unscriptural, unlawful, or immoral sexual activities
- ✓ **THE COVETOUS** : those who are greedy; fix their desires upon; and seek wider significance (Note: this can be positive if handled properly)
- ✓ **EXTORTIONERS** : those who practice robbery, seizure, or carry away by force
- ✓ **IDOLATERS**: those who worship an appearance, an idea, or a false representation of God
- ✓ **REVILERS**: those who speak evil of others or are judgmental
- ✓ **DRUNKARDS**: those intoxicated with wine or strong drink, implying wrong participation in the shedding of blood, bad habits, etc.

Any of us can fall into sin-so do not look down on your brother or sister. Rather, you are in a position to intercede in prayer for their recovery and restoration to the Lord and to His people.

A Conversation with Wisdom

EXAMPLES OF PEOPLE WHO KEPT BAD COMPANY
- ✓ Lot/ Residents of Sodom (Gen. 13:10)
- ✓ Dinah/ The Daughters of Shechem (Gen. 34:1)
- ✓ Saul/ The Witch of Endor (1 Sa. 28:7)

5.6.1 EXERCISE

Reread 1 Cor. 5:9-13. What is the main point of emphasis here? "Not to company with" is strong language. How do you interpret this?

5.6.2 EXERCISE

Read 2 Cor. 7:1, 10-11. Commit verse 1 to memory. Write it out in your own words. Can you identify the seven fruits of repentance in the above passage? Define each "fruit" in your own words: Carefulness, Clearing yourself, Indignation, Fear, Vehement desire, Zeal, Revenge. Write two paragraphs describing how you might put the preceding lesson into practice in your life.

5.7 ON A POSITIVE NOTE

Fortunately, the Bible does more than just provide us with a laundry list of people and behaviors to avoid; it tells us what kinds of people and behaviors we should have in our lives- and how to make wise choices that will push us further down the path of His glory and our good.

WE SHOULD ASSOCIATE WITH
- ✓ The Humble (Pro. 16:19)
- ✓ The Poor/ Poor in Spirit (Pro. 19:1; Mat. 5:3)
- ✓ The Faithful (Pro. 25:13)

A Conversation with Wisdom

- ✓ The Wise (Pro. 13:20)
- ✓ Worshippers (Ps. 34:3)
- ✓ True Friends (Eccl. 4:9-12)

EXAMPLES OF PEOPLE WHO KEPT GOOD COMPANY

- ✓ Daniel/ Shadrach, Meshach, Abed-Nego (Dan. 1:6-8)
- ✓ Ruth/ Naomi/ The young men and women of Boaz (Rth. 1:14-18)
- ✓ Lydia/ The Apostles (Acts 16:14-15, 40)

[**Teacher's Notes:** 1) It will be good to go into detail about the man who was expelled from the Corinthian church, also warning against the companion error of refusing to forgive and be reconciled to the brother once he repented of his wrong; 2) Compare the attitude of the older brother in the parable of the Prodigal Son. Note that separation from bad company in the world is a given in scripture, but that this portion emphasizes separation from other professing believers whose lives demonstrate a continual pattern of rebellion; and 3) Show that wisdom will let you know the timing and procedure for such separations.]

A Conversation with Wisdom

Seest thou a man diligent in his business? He shall stand before kings; He shall not stand before mean men.
Proverbs 22:29

A slack hand causes poverty, but the hand of the diligent makes rich. He that gathereth in summer is a wise son; But he that sleepeth in harvest is a son that causeth shame.
Proverbs 10:4-5

CHAPTER SIX

WISDOM @ WORK

In wisdom literature and throughout the Bible there are scriptures addressing the purpose of work, its duration, and how we are to approach it. We must do everything to the best of our abilities, in a spirit of excellence. Work is a necessary part of the human life cycle, and it will always contain an element of toil. For some, career is a source of great fulfillment and challenge; for others, tremendous stress and aggravation. Trust the Lord in your places of employment, knowing He is able to 1) shape your character in the midst of that environment; and 2) use you as salt and light in the midst of those estranged from His grace.

A Conversation with Wisdom

God often places His children in strategic positions in secular companies or in government to influence people and events for the Kingdom of God (i.e., Joseph, Nehemiah, Mordecai, Daniel, Paul). A person's place of business can also be the sphere of their ministry. That said, we cannot be too spiritual to work! The anointing will empower you and give you favor when you need it, but never expect a blessed free ride through life. This does not mean you will never make any mistakes, but it does mean that you will work conscionably with the goal of being an asset to your employer or client. We must respect our employers, show up on time, do an honest day's work, carrying ourselves with integrity.

6.1 THE THEOLOGY OF WORK

And Jehovah God took the man, and put him into the garden of Eden to dress it and to keep it. (Gen 2:15 ASV)

And unto Adam he said, Because thou hast hearkened unto the voice of thy wife, and hast eaten of the tree, of which I commanded thee, saying, Thou shalt not eat of it: cursed is the ground for thy sake; in toil shalt thou eat of it all the days of thy life; thorns also and thistles shall it bring forth to thee; and thou shalt eat the herb of the field; in the sweat of thy face shalt thou eat bread, till thou return unto the ground; for out of it wast thou taken: for dust thou art, and unto dust shalt thou return. (Gen 3:17-19 ASV)

Behold, that which I have seen to be good and to be comely is for one to eat and to drink, and to enjoy good in all his labor, wherein he laboreth under the sun, all the days of his life which God hath given him: for this is his

A Conversation with Wisdom

portion. Every man also to whom God hath given riches and wealth, and hath given him power to eat thereof, and to take his portion, and to rejoice in his labor - this is the gift of God. For he shall not much remember the days of his life; because God answereth him in the joy of his heart. (Ecc 5:18-20 ASV)

Whatsoever thy hand findeth to do, do it with thy might; for there is no work, nor device, nor knowledge, nor wisdom, in Sheol, whither thou goest. (Ecc 9:10 ASV)

whatsoever ye do, work heartily, as unto the Lord, and not unto men; knowing that from the Lord ye shall receive the recompense of the inheritance: ye serve the Lord Christ. (Col 3:23-24 ASV)

and that ye study to be quiet, and to do your own business, and to work with your hands, even as we charged you; that ye may walk becomingly toward them that are without, and may have need of nothing. (1Th 4:11-12 ASV)

For even when we were with you, this we commanded you, If any will not work, neither let him eat. For we hear of some that walk among you disorderly, that work not at all, but are busybodies. Now them that are such we command and exhort in the Lord Jesus Christ, that with quietness they work, and eat their own bread. (2Th 3:10-12 ASV)

But if any provideth not for his own, and specially his own household, he hath denied the faith, and is worse than an unbeliever. (1Ti 5:8 ASV)

A Conversation with Wisdom

Keep in mind that work includes a wide spectrum of activities-manual labor, intellectual labor, artistic engagement, volunteer services, entrepreneurship, caretaking, etc. Rather than honing in on a particular kind of work, the focus of these verses is the principle of labor and its substantive role in human life.

The Body of Christ is equipped for service by the Word, the Holy Ghost, and anointed leaders to go forth and perform our various ministries. If life requires work in the natural sense, then how much more in the spiritual sense? There is no room for apathy. However, labor in the Kingdom flows from hearts grateful for this awesome gift of salvation- we are not working to earn our acceptance with the Father. Serving God is not drudgery, but an outflow of responsive love for our Lord and Savior. Seek out opportunities to exhibit a servant's heart in your secular vocation as well.

6.1.1   EXERCISE

Have a discussion about what the foregoing verses mean. Commit at least one of these verses to memory. Pray for the work of everyone's hands to be blessed; pray for favor on jobs; pray for new careers/ training avenues for those who are currently seeking work. Pray for increased power to be salt and light at work, and for the salvation of coworkers and managers.

6.2 THE SLOTHFUL SPIRIT

Over against the Christian walking wisely at work, is the person of slothful spirit. This person believes that they are entitled to everything, and refuses to work hard. If they do work, it is done halfway and with an attitude that reflects disinterest or indifference toward the task at hand. If they do not work, they literally expect that things will come to them without having to work for it - and are generally lazy persons who think nothing of getting by at the expense of another.

A Conversation with Wisdom

Slothfulness is related to leeching, presumption, and idleness. This is an evil way of living, and should not be found among God's children. If we are well enough to work, and are in a financial position where we need to work, then we ought to be gainfully employed, whether working for others, working as a stay-at-home parent, or operating a business. A slothful person is unreliable, neglectful of their responsibilities, always taking and never giving. Thankfully, the Word of God provides a remedy for such a condition-a renewed mind in this area is a sign that breakthrough is around the corner.

6.2.1 EXERCISE

What are your thoughts on the matter? How can a renewed mind cancel a slothful outlook?

6.3 DILIGENCE AND SLOTH COMPARED

The thoughts of the diligent tend only to plenteousness; But every one that is hasty hasteth only to want. (Pro 21:5 ASV)

The soul of the sluggard desireth, and hath nothing; But the soul of the diligent shall be made fat. (Pro 13:4 ASV)

The hand of the diligent shall bear rule; But the slothful shall be put under taskwork. (Pro 12:24 ASV)

He becometh poor that worketh with a slack hand; But the hand of the diligent maketh rich. (Pro 10:4 ASV)

...in diligence not slothful; fervent in spirit; serving the Lord; (Rom 12:11 ASV)

A Conversation with Wisdom

Be diligent in these things; give thyself wholly to them; that thy progress may be manifest unto all. (1Ti 4:15 ASV)

These principles indicate that it is not always an attack of the devil that causes emptiness in the life of a believer. Is it possible that a lack of diligence lies at the root of the problem? The Lord is able and willing to impart a dynamic, effective work ethic into your life today. It begins with a readiness to change the way you think.

6.4 THE LAZY/SLOTHFUL SPIRIT DESCRIBED

- ✓ The lazy man turns on his bed like a door on a hinge (Pro. 26:14)
- ✓ The lazy man won't even work hard to feed himself (Pro. 26:15)
- ✓ The sluggard is happy to sleep his way through life (Pro. 6:9)
- ✓ Laziness causes a person to do without things they need
- ✓ Laziness opens the door to sudden poverty (Pro. 24:33-34)
- ✓ Laziness and destruction go together (Pro. 18:9)
- ✓ A lazy man talks a lot and does nothing (Pro. 14:23)
- ✓ A lazy man always has an excuse (Pro. 20:4)
- ✓ The lazy man has irrational fears that keep him from taking action (Pro. 26:13)
- ✓ The sluggard lets opportunities pass him by
- ✓ A lazy man never realizes his full potential

THE EFFECTS OF LAZINESS

I went by the field of the sluggard, And by the vineyard of the man void of understanding; And, lo, it was all grown over with thorns, The face thereof was covered with nettles,

And the stone wall thereof was broken down. Then I beheld, and considered well; I saw, and received instruction: Yet a little sleep, a little slumber, A little folding of the hands to sleep; So shall thy poverty come as a robber, And thy want as an armed man. (Pro 24:30-34 ASV)

6.4.1   EXERCISE

Write two paragraphs about your work ethic. Are you diligent? Are you slothful? Pray about areas where you have been challenged. Have faith in the grace and power of God to meet your needs as your thinking is transformed.

6.5 EMPLOYEE ATTITUDE

As the cold of snow in the time of harvest, So is a faithful messenger to them that send him; For he refresheth the soul of his masters. (Pro. 25:13 ASV)

Servants, be obedient unto them that according to the flesh are your masters, with fear and trembling, in singleness of your heart, as unto Christ; not in the way of eyeservice, as men-pleasers; but as servants of Christ, doing the will of God from the heart; with good will doing service, as unto the Lord, and not unto men: knowing that whatsoever good thing each one doeth, the same shall he receive again from the Lord, whether he be bond or free. (Eph 6:5-8 ASV)

"Eyeservice" means that work is only being done when people are watching. It's dishonest-not doing a full day's work. Furthermore, we are to do our best even when our employers are not the most amiable. Good, honest work and upright character is a better witness at work than a desk draped in Christian bumper stickers!

Consider how anointed Joseph was, causing Potiphar's estate to prosper, only to be framed by his master's wife (Gen. 39:1-6)! Yet because of his good work, Potiphar saw that the Lord was with him. Consider how anointed David was as he played the harp for Saul, only to have javelins thrown in his direction! Though Saul had an evil eye toward David, he could not help but notice two things: 1) David behaved wisely in all his affairs; and 2) The Lord was with him (1 Sa. 18:10-15).

EXAMPLES OF GOOD WORK ETHIC

Daniel is an excellent example of a man who was faithful at every stage of advancement in his life. As a young man taken into the Babylonian captivity, he refused to eat the food apportioned by the king, which likely contained things forbidden by the Law or perhaps offered to idols. God answered his commitment with blessing-allowing he and his companions to appear healthier in countenance after ten days of only vegetables and water (Dan. 1:12). All four men were chosen and elevated because of their knowledge, skill and aptitude in the natural realm-but true promotion is of the Lord, who rewards faithfulness in His children (Ps. 75:5-6).

Daniel served in positions of governmental authority under three empires-the Babylonian, Mede and Persian; and received divine revelation regarding the reign of the Greeks, Romans, and eschatological events. Throughout that time, Daniel did not allow the influences of pagan culture to crowd out his relationship with God. We see him working hard and praying hard; attending to the king's business and diligently studying the Scriptures. His life was beautifully synchronized to the timing and will of God-and there was not one scandal recorded in scripture to mar it. Consider these words:

It pleased Darius to set over the kingdom a hundred and twenty satraps, who should be

A Conversation with Wisdom

throughout the whole kingdom; and over them three presidents, of whom Daniel was one; that these satraps might give account unto them, and that the king should have no damage. Then this Daniel was distinguished above the presidents and the satraps, because an excellent spirit was in him; and the king thought to set him over the whole realm. Then the presidents and the satraps sought to find occasion against Daniel as touching the kingdom; but they could find no occasion nor fault, forasmuch as he was faithful, neither was there any error or fault found in him. Then said these men, We shall not find any occasion against this Daniel, except we find it against him concerning the law of his God. (Dan 6:1-5 ASV)

Notice the words that describe Daniel's work ethic-his integrity, excellent spirit, and (implied) administrative abilities made him a valuable asset to the king. Likewise, we ought to make ourselves valuable to the companies or individuals for whom we work. Even under close scrutiny from his enemies, Daniel walked uprightly in the assignments he was given. However, Daniel also understood that though his loyalty to the king was important, his faithfulness to the Lord was more important.

EXAMPLES OF POOR WORK ETHIC

Now the sons of Eli were base men; they knew not Jehovah. And the custom of the priests with the people was, that, when any man offered sacrifice, the priest's servant came, while the flesh was boiling, with a flesh-hook of three teeth in his hand; and he struck it into the pan, or kettle, or caldron, or pot; all that the flesh-hook brought up the priest took therewith. So

> *they did in Shiloh unto all the Israelites that came thither. Yea, before they burnt the fat, the priest's servant came, and said to the man that sacrificed, Give flesh to roast for the priest; for he will not have boiled flesh of thee, but raw. And if the man said unto him, They will surely burn the fat first, and then take as much as thy soul desireth; then he would say, Nay, but thou shalt give it me now: and if not, I will take it by force. And the sin of the young men was very great before Jehovah; for the men despised the offering of Jehovah. (1Sa 2:12-17 ASV)*

The young men did not observe the charge of the Lord, which they were commanded to keep. In fact, they despised the ordinances of God, and solicited others to do evil. Although they were serving in the tabernacle ministry, we can see that they were unfaithful in their work-having no heart to serve God's interests or lead the people in a positive direction. The consequence of their gross sin, and of Eli's failure to correct them while he was able, led to the capture of the Ark of God, the death of Eli and his sons, and the installation of Samuel as prophet of the Lord (1 Sa. 2-4).

THE LORD OUR PROVIDER

Note that not all poverty is caused by folly or laziness. It can be the result of cruel government oppression or corporate greed-or come in the aftermath of a natural disaster such as an earthquake or hurricane. There are times when the family provider takes ill or passes away, and those that remain must find a new way to live/survive. Sometimes Christians lose their property due to persecution for the faith. The list is endless. But thanks be to God, He is our Provider! The Lord will give you everything you need when you need it most, and those blessings may come in the form of cash, favor, or opportunity. In fact, there are infinite ways for the Father to bless you! So if you're employment situation is not ideal right now, don't worry! The Lord has promised to "supply all your need according to His riches in glory by Christ Jesus." (Phil. 4:19)

6.5.1   EXERCISE

Tap into your arsenal of gifts and talents. Are you able to do something that is both God-glorifying and lucrative? Seek God as to whether you can develop those skills into a business. Do you see someone with a skill or talent they do not appear to be using? Encourage them to pursue new avenues of work. Some of us just need a little push before we can dream big.

6.6 EMPLOYER ATTITUDE

Masters, render unto your servants that which is just and equal; knowing that ye also have a Master in heaven. (Col 4:1 ASV)

And, ye masters, do the same things unto them, and forbear threatening: knowing that he who is both their Master and yours is in heaven, and there is no respect of persons with him. (Eph 6:9 ASV)

Perhaps you are a manager, business owner, or corporate executive. If so, keep in mind that the Lord expects you to treat those under you with fairness, and to see that they receive just compensation for their labor. As you serve in that capacity, be mindful that you also work for someone-and He does not pick favorites. Speak to your employees sternly if and when necessary, but never behave in a threatening, abusive manner. The literal meaning of the command is to "desist from menace." Understand that it is difficult to work under such conditions, and workers are not only worthy of their hire, but deserve an atmosphere conducive to productivity.

A Conversation with Wisdom

REST

Finally, note that work must be balanced with rest. The Sabbath was established for this purpose-to signify a cessation from labor. Though the world threatens to take up every moment of the 24-hour day, we must still take time to rest, recover, and be refreshed in the Holy Ghost. We do this in corporate worship-but we can also do this daily in our prayer closets. During His earthly ministry, between crowds of thousands and the voices of His critics, the Lord Jesus often disappeared to spend time alone with the Father. He knew the priceless nature of those moments. And to those trying to live under the burden of the Law, He says:

> *Come unto me, all ye that labor and are heavy laden, and I will give you rest. Take my yoke upon you, and learn of me; for I am meek and lowly in heart: and ye shall find rest unto your souls. For my yoke is easy, and my burden is light. (Mat 11:28-30 ASV)*

[Teacher's Notes: 1) Impress on students that being a Christian does not mean that you won't have to work for a living, necessarily. Encourage good work habits and career advancement where God's glory is clearly in view; 2) Explain that while diligence brings reward, we should not overwork to be rich. This is not balance; 3) Encourage mothers who, instead of working, stay at home with their children. They are neither lazy nor unproductive, but in fact working to invest in young lives, training them up in righteousness; and

A Conversation with Wisdom

4) Some people cannot find work-encourage students to share knowledge of new employment opportunities with each other; or to make their skills available to help others get on their feet professionally.]

A Conversation with Wisdom

A Conversation with Wisdom

I have only just a minute; only 60 seconds in it, Forced upon me; can't refuse it, didn't see it, didn't choose it. But, it's up to me to use it. It's just a tiny little minute; but eternity is in it.
Katherine J. Williams

It is time to dialogue with your destiny.
Joseph N. Williams

CHAPTER SEVEN

ECCLESIASTES: THE SEARCH FOR LIFE'S MEANING

The 20th century was an unprecedented time for global innovation. We have built great weapons of war, machines for mass production, made sweeping medical advances and even traveled to the moon. We have built titanic ocean liners, narrowed the communication gap between countries, ended chattel slavery and made great strides toward women's rights. Still, the wisest man who ever lived lets us know that "there is nothing new under the sun" (Ecc. 1:9). What does he mean by this? Surely no one was flying around the globe in a private jet 3,000 years ago. Surely there was no world wide web. There weren't even antibiotics for the common infection.

King Solomon meant that although the trappings of life may change, human nature and the things we have in mind to do are static parts of an earthly life. People once gathered at the local market to learn of news from afar. Now people gather to social networking sites and can shop online while they're at it. People rode in caravans or took boats. Now people drive cars or fly aircraft. People gathered on special occasions to dance, listen to music, witness drama, or hear the latest philosophy. Today, we go to the ballet, rock concerts, Broadway plays, or a special lecture series at our city university. Now, everyone's into herbal remedies. But witch doctors go back quite a few centuries. Today, the teen book and movie market is flooded with novels about witchcraft and divination. Again, history is replete with references to such occultic indulgences - only the form has changed. There's really nothing of which it can be said, "See, this is new" (Ecc. 1:10).

7.1 OLD IS THE NEW "NEW"

The book of Ecclesiastes captures man's search for the meaning of life. In a time when technology promises great and uncharted opportunity, we must remember that according to scripture, the same patterns continue on under different labels. What really matters, and what the king takes into consideration throughout the book, is the significance of a life lived with or without God at its center.

7.1.1   EXERCISE

Review the following well-known sayings from the book of Ecclesiastes:
- a) Ecc. 1:9
- b) Ecc. 1:10
- c) Ecc. 3:1

A Conversation with Wisdom

    d)   Ecc. 12:1
    e)   Eccl 12:13

Commit at least three of these verses to memory. How do they shape your view of human life?

7.2 MAKING SENSE OF THE RAT RACE

Life runs on a seemingly endless cycle that results in human exasperation- a perpetual sense of dissatisfaction. This feeling can lead a person to believe that all of life is to no purpose at all - that it's just a "harsh existence" that's been dealt to us from above. Everything we can see, hear, know, touch, smell, taste or experience in the natural world still leaves us discontented, and understanding that there is a God who orders our lives with a deliberate purpose in mind, and to whom we must give an account of our dealings, puts everything in perspective. Nothing makes sense without Him because He puts purpose into the equation.

How did we get on this cycle of frustration to begin with - this cycle of life, death, and forgetting all that preceded us? The disruption of the balanced, fulfilled life by the entrance of sin into the world lies at the root of the problem. This is why everything in creation was plunged into futility- as discussed by the apostle Paul in Romans 8:19-23.

Throughout Ecclesiastes, the Preacher points out life's various vanities and things that vex the spirit. These are things that just don't seem to add up or make any sense, and yet, because it is the absolute order of things, we must accept that which we cannot change. Most of these expressions are directed toward ironies-working hard and then leaving one's increase to a foolish heir; living wisely, only to die the same way as the fool; or stockpiling material wealth when it's only good to look at (Ecc. 2:14, 18-19; 5:11).

A Conversation with Wisdom

Reference	Without God	Ultimately Leads To
1:7-8	Learning	Sarcasm / Pessimism
1:16-18	Greatness	Sorrow
2:1-2	Pleasure	Disappointment
2:17	Labor	Hatred of Life
3:1-9	Philosophy	Emptiness
3:11	Unsure about Life	Lack of Fulfillment
4:2-3	Life	Depression
5:12	Wealth	Unrest
6:12	Just Existing	Resignation
11:1-8	Wisdom	Despair

7.2.1 EXERCISE

Read Ecc. 1:3-11 and determine why nothing makes sense without God. Write a paragraph explaining this.

7.3 BEEN THERE, DONE THAT, GOT THE TUNIC

Solomon, by virtue of his abundant wealth, authority, and wisdom, took it upon himself to search out what way of life is best for a human being in this world. This project led him to indulge in the pleasures of the rich and of the poor, yet his wisdom remained with him (Ecc. 2:9). The repeated language, "I did this for myself," or "I got that for myself," bespeaks a preoccupation with self-satisfaction in the material realm. The pursuit was all about self-validation in a fallen world. Solomon tried everything. Among his pursuits were the following:

- ✓ The accumulation of horses (1 Ki. 4:26)
- ✓ The accumulation of gold, tribute from other rulers (1 Ki. 10:14-15)

A Conversation with Wisdom

- ✓ The accumulation of beautiful women (1 Ki. 11:3)
- ✓ The accumulation of vast properties (Ecc. 2:4-5)
- ✓ The accumulation of male/female singers for premium entertainment (Ecc. 2:8)
- ✓ The accumulation of slaves, purchased and home-born (Ecc. 2:7)
- ✓ An indulgence in alcohol (Ecc. 2:3)
- ✓ An indulgence in foolishness (Ecc. 1:17)
- ✓ Hard work (Ecc. 2:19)
- ✓ The pursuit of botanical and animal knowledge (1 Ki. 4:33)

At the end of this experiment, Solomon concluded that it was all vanity (Ecc. 12:8). Everything around abounded with futility and emptiness. No matter how one lived, he reasoned, we are all careening toward the pit of death. What could be more important than enjoying oneself now? This reasoning changes form over the course of several chapters, but he concludes that while we are enjoying the fruit of our labor during our short lives, we must "fear God and keep His commandments" (Ecc. 12:13). Not only is this our duty as human beings, but we will also be judged for our lives. This is the bottom line of life. Enjoyment in life comes only from God. This means that whatever God does not honor, we cannot honor. Pleasure can be a delight and yet a horror if God is left out.

7.4 GRASPING AT THE WIND

King Solomon laments the fact that there are those who work hard their entire lives in the pursuit of knowledge, wisdom, and equity, but after their deaths, others who have not made any such investments reap the rewards of their labor. He is allowing his heart to cry, "What's the point? What do we really get out of anything to which we painstakingly apply ourselves?"

For the average person, life is an endless litany of hard work and sorrow of heart. Further, he explains that while knowledge is good, it does not come without a price, because the more one knows, the greater his level of grief and sorrow (Ecc. 1:18; 12:12). To eat and drink in peace and simplicity, to enjoy one's labor and its fruit, are gifts from the hand of God. God blesses those who walk uprightly not only with knowledge and wisdom, but also with joy (Ecc. 2:26; 5:20).

Solomon summarized his many attempts at finding meaning in his life as "chasing the wind." We feel the wind as it passes, but we can't catch hold of it or keep it. We were created to love, worship, and know God-to spend our lives in anything else is to miss our ultimate purpose. We must remember, in all of our accomplishments, security and self-worth are found in an honest relationship with God. Think about what you consider worthwhile in your life; your time, energy, and money. Will you look back at all these and decide that these too, were "chasing the wind?"

7.4.1 EXERCISE

In Ecc. 2:1-11, Solomon speaks about "me, myself, and I." What is he really saying? Write a short essay explaining how such pursuits have affected your life. What have you learned about their value in the vast scheme of things?

7.4.2 EXERCISE

How do you describe vanity? What is the conclusion of the whole matter? Read Ecc. 2:20-24. What is Solomon's short term attitude toward pleasure? What is his long term attitude toward work? What is God's gift to us in v. 24?

A Conversation with Wisdom

7.5 TIMES AND SEASONS

In Ecclesiastes 3, we learn that life has times and seasons. There is a time and place for every natural event, and those who are wise understand this. Nothing lasts forever, but as surely as the earth turns on its axis, light and darkness follow each other in their course. Each experience and event in our lives has a purpose in God's supreme plan for our lives. He is never surprised by our circumstances. Solomon said:

> *I know that, whatsoever God doeth, it shall be for ever: nothing can be put to it, nor anything taken from it; and God hath done it, that men should fear before him. That which is hath been long ago; and that which is to be hath long ago been: and God seeketh again that which is passed away. (Ecc 3:14-15 ASV)*

God knows how to orchestrate the events of our lives according to His perfect timing. There is a difference between observing the calendar (Gk. *chromos*) and perceiving the prophetic season for a thing to take place (Gk. *kronos*). It was said that the sons of Issachar "understood the times and knew what Israel ought to do" (1 Ch. 12:32). Likewise, we should be well aware of the time and season in which God has called (and is calling) us forth to shine in Him. Meditate on the awesomeness of God's timing in the following passages:

> *And this, **knowing the season**, that already **it is time** for you to awake out of sleep: for now is salvation nearer to us than when we first believed. (Rom 13:11 ASV)*

Concerning which salvation the prophets sought and searched diligently, who prophesied of the grace that should come unto you: **searching what time or what manner of time** the Spirit of Christ which was in them did point unto, when it testified beforehand the sufferings of Christ, and the glories that should follow them. To whom it was revealed, that not unto themselves, but unto you, did they minister these things, which now have been announced unto you through them that preached the gospel unto you by the Holy Spirit sent forth from heaven; which things angel desire to look into. (1Pe 1:10-12 ASV)

> *Humble yourselves therefore under the mighty hand of God, that he may exalt you in due **time**; (1Pe 5:6 ASV)*

7.5.1　　EXERCISE

Choose five things from 3:1-8 that have taught you important lessons so far. Read Ecc. 3:14-15 again. You need to understand that your future already happened! Why does God arrange life this way? Does this mean that we no longer have responsibilities in life?

[**Teacher's Note**: 1) Expound here on the impact of the Fall on the cycle of life; the disruption of order between body, soul and spirit; the reversal of the earth's corruption by Christ in the Millennium Kingdom. **Teacher's Resources**: *Ethics* by Dietrich Bonheoffer.]

A Conversation with Wisdom

Thou wilt guide me with thy counsel, And afterward receive me to glory. Whom have I in heaven but thee? And there is none upon earth that I desire besides thee. My flesh and my heart faileth; But God is the strength of my heart and my portion for ever.
Asaph the Psalmist

Be ye free from the love of money; content with such things as ye have: for himself hath said, I will in no wise fail thee, neither will I in any wise forsake thee.
Hebrews 13:5 ASV

CHAPTER EIGHT

PRINCIPLES OF FINANCIAL WISDOM

It is imperative to develop a proper attitude toward finances as we live out our days in this physical body. The wrong attitude about money, possessions, or any kind of wealth is can be detrimental to your mental well-being and spiritual walk with God. In this chapter, we will take a long, difficult look at what we believe about money, why we believe it, and how to have our minds renewed in this area through the wisdom of God as expressed in the books of Proverbs and

A Conversation with Wisdom

Ecclesiastes. For many students, this will prove to be a life-changing assignment, as we prepare our hearts to "lay up for ourselves treasure in heaven, and not on this earth" (Mat. 6:19-21). The Bible is replete with principles and examples of godly financial wisdom, that even when applied by those in the world, yields fruit. Decide today to make the Owner, Ruler and Blesser your Chief Financial Officer as well.

8.1 DEVELOPING A STEWARD'S MINDSET

CONSIDERATION NO. 1. We own nothing. In no uncertain terms, the Bible lets us know that the Lord "owns the cattle on a thousand hills," and that "the earth is the Lord's and the fullness thereof." (Ps. 50:10-12) Not only does every material thing belong to Him, but also every living thing, whether visible or invisible. (Col. 1:16) Everything that exists does so for His exclusive pleasure and glory (Rev. 4:11). Therefore, any income that we earn, or inheritance that we receive, belongs to God, and we are merely stewards or managers of that which He has graciously allowed us to use for our benefit in earthly life (Deut. 14:22; Prov. 3:9-10; Mal. 3:10; and 1 Ti. 6:6-7).

CONSIDERATION NO. 2. Since we own nothing, and since He owns us, then we must understand that it is His sovereign right to determine where the blessings we receive are to be directed. In the Law (and preceding the Law as demonstrated by Abraham), God's people were required to give a tithe (or, one-tenth) of all that they received, back to God (Gen. 14:19-20; Lev. 27:30). Now, we know that God has no use for money - so what then, was the purpose of the tithe? It was to be stored up and used to care for those who served the Lord in the tabernacle (Num. 18:21). It was to be used in the management of the house of God. Similarly, in the church, tithes and offerings are devoted to paying for properties; taking care of ministers; meeting the needs of the widows; world missions; and other charitable purposes (1 Cor. 9:13-14; 1 Ti.

A Conversation with Wisdom

5:16-18). It is set apart as holy (sanctified) as an offering made unto the Lord (Phil. 4:18). These funds are not to be used (by the offerer) for anything else (Deut. 12:17-18). Truthfully, as grace believers, we ought to give over and above what was required under the law. The early church did this voluntarily, even selling their homes and bringing the proceeds (Acts 4:34-35). They were moved by the Holy Spirit to extraordinary acts of generosity.

CONSIDERATION NO. 3. God demands (and deserves) priority. Not only are we to give back to the Lord, but we are to make Him first in so doing. We are not to offer to the Lord that which (a) means nothing to us (or, is not sacrificial); or (b) is left over after we have attended to other things (2 Sam. 24:22-24; Hag. 1:1-12). Our giving is to be done as a sacrifice unto Him, and accompanied by a reverent, thankful, worshipful, and most importantly, cheerful attitude (2 Cor. 9:7). When we give to the Lord and to His Kingdom, we are demonstrating that we are not so attached to material wealth that we can't let go of it when called upon to do so. Faith looks at all that is needed and proclaims, "If I seek Him first, and His righteousness, everything I need will be added unto me." (Matt. 6:33)

CONSIDERATION NO. 4. Why give? Our God is a giver, and we can never out-give Him. In His love for us, He "gave His only begotten Son that whosoever believeth in Him should not perish, but have everlasting life." (Jn. 3:16) Paul exclaimed "Thanks be to God for His indescribable gift!" (2 Cor. 9:15) Jesus sent His disciples out with the message of the Kingdom, saying, "freely you have received, freely give." (Matt. 10:7-8) He became poor that we might become rich! (2 Cor. 8:9) With this in mind, we should never think of giving to the Lord's work as a burden, but rather as a privilege - a chance to reflect His gracious, giving character in our spiritual lives. For this same reason, we give to others in His name. If our brother or sister is destitute of something that they need, and

A Conversation with Wisdom

you have it in your possession, should you not give it to them? (Jas. 2:15-16) God even commanded the Israelites to leave the corners of the fields untouched so that the poor could come and glean from them. (Lev. 19:9-10; Rth. 2:7) When we give, we share in the heart of God. (Remember that Christians give lovingly, out of the overflow of what God has done for us - not to rack up points with God for doing good deeds. That is works, not grace!) We come as thankful, praise-filled people, not with a poor attitude or out of compulsion to please or be seen of men (Matt. 6:2). Sharing is fundamental to the character of the Church (Acts 4:32; Heb. 13:16)!

CONSIDERATION NO. 5. You reap what you sow. There is no shortcut to stepping out on faith and being a bountiful or generous giver. The Lord has promised that when we give to those in need, He will repay what we have given - and this is a principle of life in the Kingdom of God (Ps. 126:7; Prov. 19:17; Luke 6:38; and 2 Cor. 9:6). While this should not be our only motive in giving, it is wonderful to know that God rewards generosity toward His work and toward those less fortunate. Paul admonished the Corinthians to "excel" at giving (2 Cor. 8:7).The process is cyclical-everything we have we have received from the Lord; and the more we give, the more we receive to give. "He gives seed to the sower" (2 Cor. 9:10-12).

CONSIDERATION NO. 6. What about the other 90%? Once we have determined to give the Lord that which He claims for Himself; the question remains, how do we manage the other 90% He allows us to use? This discussion will take up the remainder of the chapter.

8.1.1   EXERCISE

Allow this lesson to challenge you. If you do not give, start giving today. If you do not tithe, learn be faithful in this area (1 Cor. 4:2). If you tithe, but could increase your offering,

A Conversation with Wisdom

seek the Lord for increased faith to do so. Do you share what you have with those in need? If not, look around your life and prayerfully consider how you might help someone financially or materially. Perhaps you are in a good position financially and can underwrite a struggling ministry or charitable organization. Take these things to prayer and make notes for your personal reference. Maybe you're already doing these things - if so, worship the Lord because He is the Owner of everything, and because the windows of heaven are opened over your life. Memorize Prov. 3:9-10.

8.2 WRONG WAYS TO THINK ABOUT MONEY & POSSESSIONS

- ✓ MYTH NO. 1. Money is security. (Prov. 11:4)
- ✓ MYTH NO. 2. Money will solve all of my problems. (Ps. 49:6-9)
- ✓ MYTH NO. 3. Money is evil. (1 Ti. 6:9-10)
- ✓ MYTH NO. 4. Hey, I've got a great get rich quick scheme. (Prov. 13:11; 20:21)
- ✓ MYTH NO. 5. I don't need to work to get money; God will just give it to me. (Eccl. 11:4; 2 Th. 3:11-12)
- ✓ MYTH NO. 6. I must do unrighteous things to get money or possessions. (Prov. 10:2)
- ✓ MYTH NO. 7. All I need is a little bit more... (Eccl. 5:10)
- ✓ MYTH NO. 8. If I don't have a lot of money, then I am not blessed. (Eph. 1:3)
- ✓ MYTH NO. 9. It's okay to charge it, even if I can't pay the bill. (Prov. 7, 27)

8.2.1   EXERCISE

What are some of the wrong ways you have thought about money? Think carefully about the references for each point above. How has your particular culture or family structure informed the ways you think about your finances? Begin to seek God for a breakthrough in areas that pose particular challenges. Mediate on Psalm 49.

8.3 RIGHT WAYS TO THINK ABOUT MONEY & POSSESSIONS

- ✓ TRUTH NO. 1. Money is a necessary tool in life. (Eccl. 7:12; 10:19)
- ✓ TRUTH NO. 2. How I relate to money can reveal the attitude of my heart. (Matt. 6:19-21)
- ✓ TRUTH NO. 3. I should preserve an inheritance for my generations that is both material and spiritual. (Prov. 13:22; 3 Jn. 1:4)
- ✓ TRUTH NO. 4. Anything we have should be shared. (2 Cor. 8:13-15)
- ✓ TRUTH NO. 5. Giving for the right reasons always results in blessing. (Prov. 11:24-26)
- ✓ TRUTH NO. 6. God is my Provider, even when I have no money. (1 Kings 17:12-14)
- ✓ TRUTH NO. 7. Money and resources should be invested in the Kingdom of God. (Matt. 6:33)

8.3.1 EXERCISE

Think positively about finances, believing that God is able to bless you in this area. Revisit your individual or family budget. Is God first in its calculations? How much is spent on entertainment? Junk food? Cell phone and text messaging costs? Is there something you can reduce or cut in order to either a) save something; b) give something; or c) invest something? Write two paragraphs about your considerations.

A Conversation with Wisdom

8.4 POWERFUL POINTS ON WEALTH MANAGEMENT

- ✓ POINT 1.   Do not overwork to be rich. (Prov. 23:4)
- ✓ POINT 2.   Learn from the ants. (Prov. 6:6-8)
- ✓ POINT 3.   Do not spend what you don't have. (2 Cor. 8:12)
- ✓ POINT 4.   Avoid taking on the debts of others. (Prov. 11:15; 17:18)
- ✓ POINT 5.   Do not drive yourself into debt (Prov. 22:27).
- ✓ POINT 6.   Do not waste money on foolishness. (Lk. 15:11-14)
- ✓ POINT 7.   Work to maintain an inheritance. (Prov. 13:22)
- ✓ POINT 8.   Keep a savings account. (Gen. 41:34-36)
- ✓ POINT 9.   Do not try to buy the blessings of God. (Acts 8:18-24)
- ✓ POINT 10. Make investments in things that matter. (Eccl. 11:1, 6)
- ✓ POINT 11. Be fair in business dealings. (Prov. 20:10, 23)
- ✓ POINT 12. Seek sound financial advice. (Prov. 15:22)
- ✓ POINT 13. Do not flaunt your wealth, or seek public praise for donations. (Matt. 6:1-4)
- ✓ POINT 14. Do not show favoritism because of wealth. (Prov. 14:20; Eccl. 9:15; Jas. 2:1-6)
- ✓ POINT 15. Pay what you owe, including your taxes. (Rom. 13:6-8)
- ✓ POINT 16. Thou shalt not steal. (Ex. 20:15; Eph. 4:28)

A Conversation with Wisdom

8.4.1 EXERCISE

Read the references provided with the above points. What lessons do you learn from the ant? Do you have sound financial advisors in your life? Are you overworking just so you can have more stuff? Are you saving money or living from check to check? Write two paragraphs about the sin of showing partiality because of wealth. How do you think the Lord feels when He sees such behavior among His children? If you are a business owner or manager, do you make sure that your employees receive fair pay for their work? Make any challenges in this lesson a matter for prayer.

8.4.2 EXERCISE

Go through your closet and determine to give one item away to someone less fortunate. Instead of choosing something well-worn (though it may be in good condition), or something that no longer appeals to you, choose an outfit that is your favorite, best, or most costly, and let it go. Write a short testimony about this experience. Memorize Acts 20:35.

8.5 A WISE ACTION PLAN

Pharaoh appointed Joseph as the Prime Minister of Egypt not only because of his ability to interpret dreams that foretold the coming of a massive famine, but also because he had the foresight and wisdom to know what to do to preserve life in the midst of it (Gen. 41:1-57). Joseph directed the nation's leader to act during the seven years of plenty by putting aside 20% of the grain in storehouses. This way, when the famine hit, they could sell the grain to the public and to surrounding nations and reap a profit. This plan saved millions of lives during seven lean years, and expanded the power and might of Egypt in the region. Everyone recognized that it was the wisdom of God at work in Joseph's plans and ideas - and he had been chosen by God to display this for His honor and glory. Do you have a wise action plan in place for today?

A Conversation with Wisdom

Recognize that the Lord is far more concerned with meeting your needs than satisfying your wants, although, if you delight yourself in Him, He will give you the desire of your heart (Ps.37:4). We should never buy what we want and beg for what we really need.

BIBLICAL EXAMPLES OF MAN'S RELATIONSHIP TO MONEY

- ✓ GIVING TO GOD: Abel, Abraham, David, Widow with Two Mites, Joanna
- ✓ GIVING OUT OF REPENTANCE/FAITH: Zaccheus; Woman with Alabaster Box
- ✓ GIVING TO CHARITY: Obadiah; Ruth; Abigail; Little Boy with Lunch; Persecuted Saints; Corinthians
- ✓ WEALTH TRANSFER: Egypt to Israel; Hamaan to Esther/Mordecai; Nabal to David; Jesus Then & Now
- ✓ STINGINESS: Nabal; Rich Young Ruler
- ✓ WASTEFUL SPENDING: Prodigal Son
- ✓ GREED: Gehazi; Rich Fool; Judas; Achan; Ananias & Sapphira
- ✓ IDOLIZING MATERIAL: Belshazzar; Israel & Golden Calf
- ✓ MONEY USED IN MANIPULATION: Balaam the Prophet; Simon the Sorcerer; Girl with spirit of Divination
- ✓ REPUDIATING WEALTH FOR RIGHTEOUS REASONS: Abraham; Moses
- ✓ SHOWING OFF WEALTH: Hezekiah, Nebuchadnezzar, Xerxes

8.5.1 EXERCISE

What is your financial "action plan?" Do you have a budget? If not, try starting on one today. A sample is provided

A Conversation with Wisdom

as an appendix to this workbook. If you are in financial straits, don't despair. There is hope-the wisdom of God comes to the rescue every time!

8.6 FAVOR WITH GOD IS BETTER THAN MONEY IN THE BANK

The story of Ruth illustrates how an economically disadvantaged young widow lived as an ethnic minority among the people of Israel (Rth. 1-4). She did not allow her precarious situation stop her from working hard-gleaning on the edges of the field-that which was left for the impoverished (Rth. 2:7). She found favor with Boaz, so much so that he commanded additional bundles of grain to be dropped for her on purpose (Rth. 2:15-16). Similarly, understand and believe that God is able to "provide all of your need according to His riches in glory by Christ Jesus," whether you've got the cash or not. Nevertheless, there is no lack in the Kingdom of God. It does not experience recession! Other miracles of financial provision include the account of the Widow's Oil (2 Ki. 4:1-7); and the Widow of Zarephath (1 Ki. 7: 9-16).

Finally, let us be mindful not to brand the gospel message concerning finances with a distinctly American capitalist slant that exploits the poor of unindustrialized nations. Though we do not hear about it every day, there are still millions of Christians living in substandard conditions, suffering government persecution for their faith and depending on the charity of the saints to survive. Let us not assume that they are in this condition due to lack of faith. Instead, let us pray for them, and then get down to kingdom business and give generously toward meeting those needs. The Spirit of Christ will not make them feel guilty for having less, but the servants of Christ can do much good by planting seeds, drilling for water, teaching to read, and other such worthy investments.

[Teacher's Notes: 1) The goal of this lesson is to have the students examine their current beliefs and practices in regards

A Conversation with Wisdom

to finances and, if changes need to be made, to encourage them in acts of faith. Explain to students that money is neither evil nor good, but necessary, and that giving is an active, vital part of their worship; 2) Explain that wealth alone is not an indicator of blessing - because there are plenty of wicked persons with abundant financial resources and stockpiles of material possessions. However, durable riches and wealth dwell with true, godly wisdom, and if we follow the principles of Scripture, we will not do without. On the other hand, God allows the wicked to store up such wealth, so He can take it away and give it to those who please Him; 3) Pray with the class that the psychological stronghold of poverty - ghetto thinking (an oppressed mindset)- will be broken off of their lives, and the lives of their families; pray that God will give them hearts abounding with loving generosity - and bring forth those who will cheerfully sow into the Kingdom of God; 4) Emphasize the importance of staying out of debt and paying bills on time; and rebuke laziness in the sense that some believe they don't need to have a job (or own a business), but that money will just come to them because they are spiritually deep; 5) For those who want further study, point them to Paul's teaching in 2 Corinthians regarding sowing and reaping; seedtime and harvest; and other kingdom principles about financial increase. Remind them that they should "prosper and be in health, even as their soul prospers" (3 Jn. 1:2.); and 6) Some students may have questions not covered in this lesson, such as, what if they are married and their spouse refuses to consent to tithing/ or is not a believer at all? Or what if I am living on a fixed income, and need every dollar I have? Or, what can I give to God if I have no income at the present time? What about gambling/playing Lotto? What does the Bible say about claiming bankruptcy? Discuss the difference between actual external oppression and having an oppressed mindset. Be prepared to answer difficult questions on such topics.]

A Conversation with Wisdom

A Conversation with Wisdom

These things write I unto thee, hoping to come unto thee shortly; but if I tarry long, that thou mayest know how men ought to behave themselves in the house of God, which is the church of the living God, the pillar and ground of the truth.
Paul the Apostle

CHAPTER NINE

DISCERNING TIME AND JUDGMENT

Ecclesiastes 8: 5 teaches us an important truth. Responsible people often look for those who can solve problems, not present them with new ones. You will be more effective in your life if you learn good timing and judgment. This means being sensitive and knowing "what" needs to happen, "when" it needs to occur, and "how" something can be accomplished. Often the success or failure of an endeavor is linked to one's sense of timing and judgment. Understanding is the great companion to all true wisdom (Pro. 4:7). In this chapter, we will focus on the whats, whens and hows of the wise life.

A Conversation with Wisdom

Who so keepeth the commandment shall know no evil thing; and a wise man's heart discerneth time and judgment: (Ecc 8:5 ASV)

<u>DISCERNMENT</u>: perception, knowledge, observation with recognition of key elements or distinguishing factors.

<u>TIME</u>: a conceptual tool used to measure the continuity of existence or lack thereof; a keen understanding of appropriateness based on all factors influencing a particular moment.

<u>JUDGMENT</u>: a verdict, sentence of law, right, privilege, or penalty administered.

9.1 TIME AS CONCEPT

Time stands in contrast to eternity. Eternity has no beginning and no end, but rather stretches infinitely in all directions. When we say that something is everlasting, a finite beginning point is implied - but there is no end in sight to its existence. Another word for everlasting is "forever." Consider God placing a protractor at a point in eternity and carving out a circle called time. Then within that circle, place the linearities of all life: human, animal, sentient. This life is only a section - a minimal portion of the true life that ever was and always will be. Remember: the flesh is bound by the laws of time and space, but the spirit realm and all that pertains thereto is not. We are spirits enclosed in physical bodies. This is why it is of utmost importance that we live our lives for the glory and honor of God, because the decision we make about His Son will determine where we will spend eternity.

When God created our first parents, He designed them to live forever. Even today, when we get cuts on our fingers, microscopic resources rush to the site of the injury, slowing the damage and repairing the skin. Our immune system is made to fight off infections and the presence of foreign bodies. However, the entrance of sin, and its consequence of death, means that even in the best of health, we will ultimately die. Some die at 1, others at 10, still others at 100. But time is

A Conversation with Wisdom

always of the essence! It is not to be taken for granted - it is something that must be redeemed. None of us knows how many years we have on this earth. Consider the prayer of Moses, a man who lived 120 years and died in optimum physical and mental condition:

> A prayer of Moses the man of God. Lord, thou hast been our dwelling-place In all generations. Before the mountains were brought forth, Or ever thou hadst formed the earth and the world, Even from everlasting to everlasting, thou art God. Thou turnest man to destruction, And sayest, Return, ye children of men. For a thousand years in thy sight Are but as yesterday when it is past, And as a watch in the night. Thou carriest them away as with a flood; they are as a sleep: In the morning they are like grass which groweth up. In the morning it flourisheth, and groweth up; In the evening it is cut down, and withereth. For we are consumed in thine anger, And in thy wrath are we troubled. Thou hast set our iniquities before thee, Our secret sins in the light of thy countenance. For all our days are passed away in thy wrath: We bring our years to an end as a sigh. The days of our years are threescore years and ten, Or even by reason of strength fourscore years; Yet is their pride but labor and sorrow; For it is soon gone, and we fly away. Who knoweth the power of thine anger, And thy wrath according to the fear that is due unto thee? So teach us to number our days, That we may get us a heart of wisdom. Return, O Jehovah; How long? And let it repent thee concerning thy servants. Oh satisfy us in the morning with thy loving kindness, That we may rejoice and be glad all our days. Make us glad according to the days wherein thou hast afflicted us, And the years wherein we have seen evil. Let thy work appear unto thy servants, And thy glory upon their children. And let the favor of the Lord our God be upon us; And establish thou the work of our hands upon us; Yea, the work of our hands establish thou it. (Psa. 90:1-17 ASV)

A Conversation with Wisdom

9.1.1 THINKING

Take a few moments and reflect on the brevity of life and the importance of redeeming (buying back at one's expense) the time we are given. Are you using your time wisely? If not, what changes can you make to show your acceptance of Moses' attitude toward time?

9.1.2 EXERCISE

Fill in the blanks on the following chart. Two have already completed as examples.) For each principle, write whether it relates to knowing "how," "when," or "what" to do something. What do you learn from thinking through everyday choices in this manner?

A Conversation with Wisdom

THINKING THINGS THROUGH

Scripture Reference	Seed, Cause, or Action	Fruit, Effect, or Result	In Your Own Words
Pro. 24:10	Little strength	Fainting in the day of adversity	
Pro. 24:17-18	Don't rejoice when your enemy falls or is overthrown	It displeases the Lord, who may remove His anger from him	
Pro. 24:27	First prepare your work in the field	Then go and build your house	
Pro. 25:8	Don't be in a hurry to stir up strife	You won't know what do when your neighbor embarrasses you	Know how to choose your battles.
Pro. 25:17	Don't go to your neighbor's house often	Lest he grow weary of you and hate you	Know when to leave.
Pro. 25:20	Don't sing to a heavy heart	It's like taking away someone's coat in winter	
Gal. 6:9	Don't be weary in well doing. If you don't faint	In due season you will reap	

A Conversation with Wisdom

9.2 TIMING IS EVERYTHING

Solomon's poem on the times and seasons teaches us that there is an appropriate time for everything that happens in this life. More than that, there are certain behaviors or courses of action that are only appropriate at certain times. A wise person will move in accordance with appropriate time and season. (On the same note, it may appear to be one time in the natural realm, when God can decree a shift in season, making it time for something completely different. When this happens, only those with ears to hear what the Spirit is saying to the churches will truly know what time it is.)

A farmer doesn't plant seeds in winter and wait for harvest in spring. He understands the seasons and knows that certain actions will be unfruitful at certain times. Similarly, when someone is suffering, it is not the time to sing and make joyful melody - but to offer comfort and a listening ear. Consider Solomon's poem in its entirety:

> *For everything there is a season, and a time for every purpose under heaven: a time to be born, and a time to die; a time to plant, and a time to pluck up that which is planted; a time to kill, and a time to heal; a time to break down, and a time to build up; a time to weep, and a time to laugh; a time to mourn, and a time to dance; a time to cast away stones, and a time to gather stones together; a time to embrace, and a time to refrain from embracing; a time to seek, and a time to lose; a time to keep, and a time to cast away; a time to rend, and a time to sew; a time to keep silence, and a time to speak; a time to love, and a time to hate; a time for war, and a time for peace. (Ecc. 3:1-8 ASV)*

We can learn to face the realities of life. Read Hebrews 4: 14-16. Write your thoughts on this. Define the following terms: foresight; insight; hindsight. How have you learned from these? Write a brief essay about this.

9.3 A WORD ON TIME MANAGEMENT

In our fast paced society, good time management skills have become essential to the attainment of a balanced life. Most of us make use of planning tools, such as calendars or scheduling software, to keep track of important dates, times, and obligations. Do you have a planner? If not, consider investing in one. That said, it is also possible to take planning and scheduling too far. We should always be mindful that:

- ✓ Whatever we plan to do will only take place "Lord willing." To boast as if tomorrow were promised is evil (Jas 4:15).
- ✓ Don't worry about tomorrow. Each day has enough trouble of its own. Face tomorrow by faith (Mat. 6:34)
- ✓ Whatever we plan to do, must be done to the glory and honor of God (i.e., no sinful activities) (Col. 3:17).
- ✓ We cannot leave God out of our plans, but must have time for prayer and reading of God's word (Jos. 1:8; Eph. 6:18).
- ✓ We cannot leave God's people out of our plans, but must make time for fellowship with one another (Heb. 10:25).
- ✓ At times, life throws unexpected curves that cause plans to change without notice (Ecc. 9:11).

OTHER PRIORITIES OF LIFE INCLUDE:
- ✓ Home/Family
- ✓ School/Work
- ✓ Community/Ministry

- ✓ Personal Time, Rest/Leisure

9.4 THE WELL-TIMED LIFE

The foremost example of a life governed by good timing is the Lord Jesus. Although He was the lamb slain from the foundations of the world, yet He did not manifest Himself in flesh until "the fullness of time" had come (Gal. 4:4). Why did it take 42 generations for Him to appear on the earth? Why didn't He just come to die for our sins right after the Fall? It isn't long before we realize that timing and purpose are closely related. For it was His plan to bring many sons to glory, not just a few (Heb. 2:10). It was His plan to restore His image in millions--billions of believers down through the ages, and what a privilege it is to be in the number. During His earthly life and ministry, He operated in accordance with the timetable of God, led by the Holy Spirit into every parable, miracle, and movement. The events of His death, burial and resurrection were executed with precision - so that He was offered up between two evenings, our Passover Lamb (1 Cor. 5:7). Matthew's gospel is full of verses that say "this happened that it might be fulfilled." Nothing was left to chance.

The lives of the apostles were also governed by the Spirit and timing of God. When they wanted to move in one direction, dreams, visions, prophecies, and angelic visitations prompted them to move in a different way. This usually resulted in an opportunity to preach to those they would never have met otherwise, with amazing results (Acts 16:7-10).

Only the person whose spirit is attuned to the voice of God and the heart of God will be receptive to His timing. That is why we are told to wait on the Lord, as opposed to rushing into a decision without careful prayer. One of the most important lessons we will ever learn is that God's timing is not our timing. There are occasions, such as the death of Lazarus, where we are prone to accuse Him of lateness. Martha said, "Lord, if you had been here, my brother had not died" (Jn. 11:21, 32). But Jesus was right on time to demonstrate to the crowd His power over death and corruption. So we may misunderstand when God wants to do some things in our lives. Remember that just because it takes a while, doesn't mean His answer is no.

Sometimes, prophetic individuals like Daniel, does understand some aspect of God's timing. Like Daniel, we are to set our prayers in agreement with His Word and purpose at that moment. The Holy Spirit is there to help us in our prayers (Rom. 8:26).

9.5 TRUE DISCERNMENT VS. "ANOINTED SUSPICION"

Paul and the apostles were walking through Philippi and a slave girl began following them and shouting "These men are servants of the most high God who proclaim unto you the way of salvation" (Acts 16:11-20, ASV). There are several things happening at this moment. Paul finds himself in the midst of a city wholly devoted to polytheism and idolatry, particularly prone to demonic magical arts. He discerns this in his spirit, that is, he can tell that though her statement is true, the spirit behind the statement is false; and through its prediction of events, would continue to bind people to a dependence on divination, being accepted as authoritative. (Note that discernment or judgment of a thing is not the same as "anointed suspicion." Just because you are suspicious doesn't mean you are correct!) Paul knew the story of Saul and the witch at Endor (1 Sa. 28:7). He know that the Lord Jesus had no need for the testimony of demons (Luk. 4:41). Therefore he turned in vexation and cast out the evil spirit. This resulted in:

- ✓ The power of Christ being displayed
- ✓ Liberation of the slave girl
- ✓ The cancellation of a demonic stronghold over a city

A Conversation with Wisdom

- ✓ The imprisonment of the apostles

9.6 MEETING LIFE'S CHALLENGES INEFFECTIVELY

It is not only important that we learn good timing and judgment, but also that we learn to meet life's challenges effectively. When we don't respond to situations in appropriate ways, we can lose our sensitivity to the timing at work in our lives or abandon sound judgment. Three common ways of responding ineffectively to life's challenges are escapism (running from challenge); denial (behaving as if no challenge exists) and indifference (not caring about anything).

ESCAPISM

Jonah the prophet was confronted by a command to go to Nineveh and cry out against its great wickedness. He felt challenged because he did not want God to have mercy on the people there. He wanted to see them punished, or at best, left to themselves. Instead of humbling himself and seeking a right heart on the matter; going forward in obedience, he ran away. Running away from life's issues does not solve anything. Very often, the storms of life will increase because in reality, you cannot hide from God. Jonah's season of escapism landed him on a boat going in the opposite direction of his assignment. Yet even in this, he was used by the Lord (ref.). God had to put Jonah in a place that would press him to realize his obligation to the Word of the Lord. Later, God showed him the error of his thoughts regarding the Ninevites, but Jonah was adamant about his opinions.

INDIFFERENCE

Cain was a farmer who worked hard all of his life to cultivate the earth. When the time came to present an offering, he decided to give God his very best-the fruit of the ground.

Cain knew from his parents that blood sacrifice was required to approach the Lord God, but he still believed that God would appreciate his effort. When God rejected his offering, He reminded Cain that he should do things correctly, and so receive the blessing. (Ref.) Instead of doing this, Cain displayed a series of ineffective responses to the challenge:

- ✓ Depression - He went away from God's presence in sadness.
- ✓ Anger - "Why didn't He accept it? I worked hard!"
- ✓ Jealousy - against Abel for bringing the blood sacrifice and receiving acceptance.
- ✓ Murder - His attitude escalated to wiping out another human life.
- ✓ Indifference - "Am I my brother's keeper?"

OTHER INEFFECTIVE WAYS TO MEET LIFE'S CHALLENGES

- ✓ Controlled by fear
- ✓ Walking in denial/unbelief
- ✓ Blame Shifting
- ✓ Inactivity/Inappropriate silence

9.7 MEETING LIFE'S CHALLENGES EFFECTIVELY

We can learn to meet the challenges of life under the sun in effective, God-glorifying ways. This is done through the various ministries of the Holy Spirit in our lives, as we give up resistance and daily choose the path of surrender and obedience. The Lord Jesus demonstrated surrender as He prayed in the Garden of Gethsemane.

A Conversation with Wisdom

COURAGE AND PRAYERFULNESS

Hadassah of Benjamin could have settled into her posh lifestyle as queen and thought nothing of saving her own neck. Yet because she feared God and obeyed the voice of her wise cousin Mordecai, she knew that she must act to save the lives of her people (Ref.). It is clear that she was afraid, but she was courageous in her determination to do what was right - demonstrated by her famous words, "I will go to the king, which is against the Law, and if I perish, I perish!" However, she did not act on this courage immediately, but humbled herself in three days of fasting, enlisting the spiritual support of those she would help, and those within her circle (Ref.). She went in, but she went in the strength of the Lord, armed with a plan divinely revealed to her heart. When we face challenges that seem to threaten our very lives, we go onward in the strength of Christ, who promises to strengthen us for our varied life assignments (Ref.).

WISDOM AND UNDERSTANDING

Daniel was taken into captivity under the Babylonians and lived until the reign of Cyrus King of Persia. He was eager to see Israel return to their own land. Throughout his illustrious career in Gentile government, he spent his time reading the Scriptures and seeking God's face. Daniel's heart was so in tune with God's, that when he understood (from reading the book of Jeremiah) that the time for Israel's captivity was quickly approaching; he set himself to intense periods of fasting and prayer. Rather than attempting to manipulate the situation through his powerful position or access, he understood that he was dealing with forces much larger than any he could control.

BOLD FAITH

Stephen, the first martyr of the church, had a reputation for speaking boldly to his adversaries with faith and wisdom

A Conversation with Wisdom

(ref.). However, one sermon about the power and authority of Christ, and the stubbornness of Israel, provoked his listeners to uncontrolled rage, and they began railing against him. He didn't run from them-he didn't hide. Instead, even with his last breath, Stephen turned his attention upward to the Lord and received a revelation powerful enough to distract him from dying. Nothing could silence his proclamation of the truth of the gospel. He cried out, "I see the heavens opened, and the Son of Man standing at the right hand of God!" This enraged the people so that they began to stone him, but Stephen was busy calling on God - even asking God not to hold their actions against them (Ref). Do you have this bold faith in the face of challenge today? Can you go as far as laying down your life for the One who gave His all those years ago?

OTHER EFFECTIVE WAYS TO MEET LIFE'S CHALLENGES

- ✓ With wisdom and understanding
- ✓ With prayerfulness
- ✓ With hope/expectation

9.7.1 EXERCISE

We can learn to face the realities of life effectively. Read Heb. 4:14-16. What are your thoughts on the availability of well-timed help? Write a brief essay to explain.

9.7.2 EXERCISE

What are some life challenges that you try to:
a) Escape?
b) Deny?
c) Handle with indifference?

How will you handle them differently as a result of this lesson?

A Conversation with Wisdom

[Teacher's Notes: 1) The topic of timing can be expanded by tracing biblical characters movements in relation to a previously spoken prophetic word, as in the cases of Esther or Joseph (NT), Cyrus, et al.; or by selecting specific moments when key events coincided, as with the Jericho march; the Day of Pentecost and the birth of the church; or Jesus' approach to the hour of His death. In the case of Joseph, observe how he was positioned in the right place at the right time, and also had the wisdom to do what was necessary. Compare this to the church today, and those who are gifted with wisdom and discernment; 2) Remind students that wisdom is available to us for the asking; and 3) There is a scripture that says Christians don't need to worry about times and seasons, but it falls within the context of eschatology. For advanced students, explain the difference between times and seasons in the end-time prophetic sense and the everyday sense of life under the sun.]

A Conversation with Wisdom

"Who you hang out with determines your character; who you lay down with determines what you produce."
Joseph N. Williams

CHAPTER TEN

SELECTING YOUR CABINET

There are two sets of people who can influence your destiny in powerful ways, with either positive or negative results. These are our "friends" and "advisers." A nation can rise or fall because of corruption among the king's advisers; a teenager can make a series of wrong choices when led to follow "friends" down the path to destruction. Good friends, like the four who helped the paralytic down through a roof to see Jesus, can further you on the road to purpose. Good advisers can keep someone from making a choice they might later regret.

Fortunately, we are not left to find our friends through trial and error, but have in scripture a wealth of information on how to make and keep positive relationships going, while avoiding and cancelling negative and potentially dangerous relationships already in our lives.

This chapter explores both illustrations and principles, and the exercises should aid the student in making wiser choices in the realm of selecting friends and advisers.

10.1 INDEPENDENCE AND ISOLATION

The old adage says, "no man is an island." This means that people exist as an interconnected network of beings, and that life cannot be lived to any degree of effectiveness in total isolation from others.

> *And five of you shall chase a hundred, and a hundred of you shall chase ten thousand; and your enemies shall fall before you by the sword. (Lev 26:8 ASV)*
>
> *He that separateth himself seeketh his own desire, And rageth against all sound wisdom. (Pro 18:1 ASV)*
>
> *Two are better than one, because they have a good reward for their labor. For if they fall, the one will lift up his fellow; but woe to him that is alone when he falleth, and hath not another to lift him up. Again, if two lie together, then they have warmth; but how can one be warm alone? And if a man prevail against him that is alone, two shall withstand him; and a threefold cord is not quickly broken. (Ecc 4:9-12 ASV)*

If we are not careful, the circumstances of life (i.e., bad experiences in prior friendships or relationships) can harden us to the point where isolation seems like the sure-fire way to avoid future heartbreak. Yet this is not true. It is by design that

A Conversation with Wisdom

we feel the need to connect with others, to share experiences, to learn about new ways of seeing the world.

In creation, God declared that it was "not good" for man to be alone. This connection is not limited to marital companionship, though it certainly starts there, but includes many aspects of interactivity between people: friendships, family relationships, professional relationships, and spiritual fellowship. People depend on each other for services, support, or to share a common interest or life goal.

One may be "independent" in the sense that they have no choice but to work for themselves, pay their own way in life, or live on their own. Yet such people usually have an external network of support to which they go for personal contact, even if it's an online community group for singles.

Many people take pride in their independence to the point where they feel they don't need anyone. Independence can cross the line into isolation when someone feels that they no longer want or need to interact with others unless absolutely necessary. This is unwise thinking. Having people in your life results in:

- ✓ Greater Productivity (Ecc. 4:9)
- ✓ Access to Assistance (Ecc. 4:10)
- ✓ Human Comfort (Ecc. 4:11)
- ✓ Security (Ecc. 4:12)
- ✓ The Ability to Share Yourself with Others

Consider the words of the Apostle Paul on the matter of independence.

> *Nevertheless, neither is the woman without the man, nor the man without the woman, in the Lord. For as the woman is of the man, so is the man also by the woman; but all things are of God. (1Co 11:11-12 ASV)*
>
> *And whether one member suffereth, all the*

members suffer with it; or one member is honored, all the members rejoice with it. Now ye are the body of Christ, and severally members thereof. (1Co 12:26-27 ASV)

10.1.1   EXERCISE

Read Ecc. 4:12. Explain in your own words. Write 2 paragraphs about a time when you were tempted to go into isolation and how you came out of it.

10.2 "FRIEND, WHY HAVE YOU COME?"

We should take great care in whom we call friends. Some people you know are "acquaintances" and must not be considered as friends. Remember, good friends are hard to find. If you have one or two, you are truly blessed.

There are times in the process of maturation that we may encounter a Judas (someone who claims to be with us but is really against us) or a Peter (someone who truly loves us but may not fully understand our purpose). In the case of these two, the enemy actually aided in the fulfillment of destiny; the friend, though well-meaning, would have hindered this.

10.2.1   EXERCISE

Write a short letter to your children (or someone else's) teaching them how to do choose their friends at school.

10.3 WHAT DO YOU KNOW?

A wise person never spends all of his time with people who only know what he knows. Wisdom will put a person in the position of always looking to learn new things, as well as admitting to what he does not know, and submitting to the authority of someone who has more knowledge of a subject. We can see this play out in our daily lives as lawyers, doctors, and politicians constantly avail themselves of academic or professional experts to fill them in on areas with which they are unfamiliar.

Surrounding yourself with people who know more than you will force you to stretch in all areas of life. If this is true in the natural realm, it is surely true in the spiritual realm. If your circle of friends is made up of disciplined students of the scriptures, it will show in their conversation, and you will inevitably learn a portion of what they know, as well as be personally challenged to come up higher in your walk with God.

In the world, this concept is called networking. But business is done differently in the kingdom of God. What is the difference? In the former, people will use a person because of what they know, without necessary regard for the individual - the purpose of meeting and sharing is almost always exploitative: what's in it for me? For the believer, everything we do should be done from pure motives, and while we are all to share our gifts and ministries with each other, there should always be an undergirding sense of love and fellowship--a desire for our mutual edification.

10.4 THE VETTING PROCESS

Presidential advisers put White House staffing candidates through a rigorous investigative process called "vetting" before appointing anyone to high public office in a new administration. This ensures that the people they select do not pose significant risks to their image and agenda. Vetting is critical because a mistake in this process can lead to the wrong people having the ear of the nation's leader, able to advise him on pertinent decisions that affect the entire population.

Likewise, the Bible provides us with something like a vetting process for potential advisers in our lives - it is a privilege to have someone's ear and a blessing to have positive people speak divine truth into or over your life. Here are some pointers to help you in the weighing process:

A Conversation with Wisdom

- ✓ Choose advises carefully (12:6, 13: 20)
- ✓ Beware of rumors and gossip-especially when it concerns a trusted friend (16:28)
- ✓ Look for people who will honor confidences (17:9)
- ✓ Check for integrity and courtesy (22:11, 27:9)
- ✓ Avoid opinions of 'angry' people (22:24)
- ✓ True friends will tell you the truth (27:6)

10.4.1 EXERCISE

Read Prov. 9:9. Write it out. What does this mean to you? How do you select advisers and evaluate what they have to say?

A Conversation with Wisdom

For this cause I also, having heard of the faith in the Lord Jesus which is among you, and the love which ye show toward all the saints, cease not to give thanks for you, making mention of you in my prayers; that the God of our Lord Jesus Christ, the Father of glory, may give unto you a spirit of wisdom and revelation in the knowledge of him…
Paul the Apostle

CHAPTER ELEVEN

LINKING OUR GOALS TO GOD'S PURPOSE

The bookstores are overrun with books offering to teach us the secrets of success. They tell us how to set goals, how to meet influential people, how to get rich quick by following a few simple rules. Most of the time, these books are found in the section called "Self Help." In the kingdom of God, where we are interested in doing business God's way, our lives are not centered around finding the best means of self-promotion. Instead, we want to develop ourselves so that we are prepared for every well-timed opportunity to be used in His service.

We believe that we can do all things, yes, but it does not stop there. We are only able to do "all things through

Christ, who strengthens us." This is important - we need to understand what success is, what the proper means are to obtaining it, and most importantly, that since our lives are not our own, without Him we can do nothing.

Wisdom will enable us to determine the path of life upon which our lives are set, and to plan in accordance with what we understand that path to entail. Of course, "many are the plans of a man's heart, but the Lord directs His steps." So we understand that plans are subject to change. However, it is very unwise to approach life without laying down goals, taking the courage to dream, and pursuing "good success" through a life of faith and obedience to the principles of scripture. The key is to make these plans prayerfully, linking our goals to God's plan. This is what growth and maturity in life is all about.

11.1 IT'S ALL ABOUT PERSPECTIVE

In Ecclesiastes, Solomon taught us about "life under the sun." Life beyond the sun, or eternity, looks entirely different. What is ordained from the foundations of the earth can appear to the eyes of man to be only an interesting coincidence.

In the same way that all truth is parallel, it is also true that no two aspects of the truth are contradictory. Most of the time these apparent contradictions can be resolved by considering the writer's perspective. In other cases, we must relegate the answers to the category of mystery, and declare that "those things which are hidden belong to the Lord our God, but that which is revealed belongs unto us and unto our children, that we may do all the words of this law." (Deu. 29:29.) In other words, I may not fully understand it, but I've still got to abide by it.

We make choices every day, and live through their varied consequences. We succeed at some things and fail miserably at others. However, it is important to realize that our actions do not stop God's plans from coming to pass, although He might change His methods and decide to use someone else.

A Conversation with Wisdom

We deal in the here and now. He deals in ultimates. A wise person keeps before his eyes at all times the absolute power, knowledge and sovereignty of God over all things and all men. He does whatever He likes, whenever He chooses, for His own glory (Ps. 115:3).

The fact of the divine predestination does not abdicate us from human responsibility. It is built into the fabric of human existence. There are at least nine reasons why we cannot sit back and wait for God to do everything for us without expending any personal effort:

- ✓ Because faith without works is dead, being alone (Jas. 2:26)
- ✓ Because we must work out our salvation with fear and trembling (Php. 2:12)
- ✓ Because we are to be doers of the work, and not hearers only (Jas. 1:22)
- ✓ Because we are to walk in that which was prepared beforehand (Eph. 2:10)
- ✓ Because we will be held accountable for our actions (2 Cor. 5:10)
- ✓ Because if we refuse, we can be replaced by someone else (Est. 4:14)
- ✓ Because it is He who works in us, both to will and to do His good pleasure (Php. 2:13)
- ✓ Because we must be diligent to make our calling and election sure (2 Pe. 1:10)
- ✓ Because He has decided that we must actively participate in our own development

11.1.1   EXERCISE

Read 3:14. At first glance it may seem to suggest that nothing people do really matters. As if God's will is ultimately going to be done and nothing may be added to it or taken away. So why not just wait for Him to do everything? Write a one page essay about this.

A Conversation with Wisdom

11.1.2 EXERCISE

Write down some of your goals, dreams, and skills. Which of these are your own ideas, and which are you certain fit into God's plan for your life in the near or distant future? How does Ecclesiastes an invitation to link your goals with God's designs? Why does God call us to personal relationship with Him?

11.1.3 EXERCISE

Name five things to place value upon while as mature in the things of God.
a)   Proverbs 15:16
b)   Proverbs 16:8
c)   Proverbs 16: 19
d)   Proverbs 17:1
e)   Proverbs 28:6

A Conversation with Wisdom

Death and life are in the power in the tongue; those who love it will eat its fruit.
Proverbs 18:21

Out of the same mouth proceedeth blessing and cursing. My brethren, these things ought not so to be.
James the Apostle

CHAPTER TWELVE

THE ART OF SPEAKING WISELY

One of the most challenging areas of our new walk with God is learning how to speak wisely. Words are incredibly powerful - possessing the ability to bless or to curse, to shift spiritual atmospheres, to promote healing or sow seeds of malice and destruction. In the world, following the desires of the carnal nature, many of us spoke whatever came into our minds - without regard for those we spoke to or the consequences of what we said. Now that we are submitted to the authority of the Scriptures and the molding of the Holy Ghost, our minds are being transformed and we recognize that

A Conversation with Wisdom

what we say must be characterized by love, grace, truth, and wisdom.

James taught that the untamed tongue is poisonous, dangerous, and spreads damage like a wildfire (Jas. 3:5-6). The Lord Jesus taught that what is in the heart of a man comes out through his mouth, and is a source of defilement (Mat. 15:11). The words that we speak will also be brought into judgment (Mat. 12:36). Therefore, it is very important that we take heed to wisdom in this matter of what we say, to whom, and how. It's glorifying to God, good for us, and beneficial to others as well. Begin by praying Psalm 19:14:

> *"Let the words of my mouth and the meditation of my heart be acceptable in Thy sight; O Lord, my strength, and my Redeemer."*

12.1 PRINCIPLES GOVERNING THE SPEECH OF THE WISE

- ✓ He knows when to speak, and when to be silent.
- ✓ He does not sing songs to a heavy heart.
- ✓ He does not laugh at his enemy's downfall.
- ✓ He does not wrong his neighbor and then say, "I was only joking."
- ✓ When he speaks, his words promote health.
- ✓ He does not answer a matter before hearing the entire story.
- ✓ He does not go around as a talebearer, separating friends.
- ✓ He keeps confidences.
- ✓ He does not boast of himself before officials/leaders, but waits to be recognized.
- ✓ He does not curse his parents.
- ✓ A wise wife does not continually nag her husband.
- ✓ A virtuous woman's speech is characterized by kindness.
- ✓ He can rejoice in giving the correct answer.

A Conversation with Wisdom

- ✓ He answers softly, turning away wrath.
- ✓ He answers a fool according to his folly, when appropriate.
- ✓ He refuses to answer a fool according to his folly, when appropriate.
- ✓ He speaks life, not death.
- ✓ He knows how to speak a word in season to him that is weary.
- ✓ He can give a good word to make a sad heart glad.
- ✓ He speaks truth.
- ✓ He does not meddle in arguments that don't concern him.
- ✓ He praises and blesses the Lord with his words daily.
- ✓ He edifies the saints, and speaks words of faith.
- ✓ He speaks to God's people about the Lord.
- ✓ He boasts in the Lord, and praises Him, not himself.

12.1.1   EXERCISE

Write two short paragraphs about a time when you said something you wish you could take back. Though you cannot take words back after they are spoken, what else should you do if you are able?

EXAMPLES OF WISE SPEECH

- ✓ Abigail to David when she met him with gifts

A Conversation with Wisdom

12.2 PRINCIPLES GOVERNING THE SPEECH OF THE UNWISE

- ✓ He speaks whatever comes to his mind, without thinking.
- ✓ He slanders his neighbor.
- ✓ He goes around as a talebearer, destroying friendships.
- ✓ He entices/invites others to do evil.
- ✓ He does evil, and then calls it a joke.
- ✓ He curses his parents.
- ✓ He covers inner hatred with smooth words.
- ✓ He talks too much - there is an overabundance of words.
- ✓ He speaks death, not life.
- ✓ He discourages others about God's power and promises.
- ✓ His mouth calls for blows.
- ✓ He makes his lack of understanding known.
- ✓ His anger, and thus angry words, are out of control.
- ✓ He makes rash vows to God, and later cannot keep them.
- ✓ He is always minding someone else's business.
- ✓ Speaks perversely.
- ✓ An unwise wife's words are nagging and contentious.

EXAMPLES OF UNWISE SPEECH

- ✓ The Ten spies who came back with a bad report

WATCH OUT FOR

- ✓ Profanity!
- ✓ Perverse Speech!

- ✓ Cruel, unkind speech!
- ✓ Provoking speech!
- ✓ Gossip and backbiting!

WE SHOULD BE:

- ✓ Quick to Listen
- ✓ Slow to Speak
- ✓ Slow to Wrath
- ✓ Bold when speaking about Christ/sharing the gospel
- ✓ Prepared to give an answer about our hope/faith

OTHER ADMONITIONS REGARDING SPEECH

- ✓ Speak as the oracles of God
- ✓ Speak according to what we believe (our faith)
- ✓ Speak the truth in love
- ✓ Impart grace to your listeners
- ✓ Speak wisdom among those who are mature
- ✓ Alcoholism/Substance Abuse promotes foolish speech and behavior

12.3   TALK LESS, PRAY MORE

All of us have said something we regret at one time or another. "Out of the abundance of our hearts, the mouth speaks" (Mat. 12:34). Maybe we spoke before thinking the matter through, or responded to something before knowing the whole story. We can do great damage by speaking in the heat of our anger - or keeping our feelings in for so long that they explode in inappropriate outbursts. As a rule, we should spend more time speaking to the Father than we do speaking to men.

The psalmist vowed to keep a guard over his mouth - and a fool evidences himself by talking too much to the wrong people about the wrong things. Christians should not be known for foul or perverse language, slander, gossip, lying, or coarse jesting; but rather for edification and truth, gloriously wound up in the grace of Christ Jesus. How does your speech hold up to the light? It is easy to watch your tongue in the company of the saints, but how about at home, on the bus, or in the subway?

12.4 FOLLOW JESUS' EXAMPLE

The Lord Jesus earthly life was one of perfect balance. He never spoke out of turn, never too harshly, too softly, nor did he ever sugar-coat his message to please his enemies. He lived perfectly before the Father, having an upright heart - and an upright heart will produce words of truth and unhindered spiritual power. He knew when to be silent, and when to say just a few choice words. All of this was possible because He walked in complete fellowship with the Father, knowing who He was and what He came to do. His words were aptly chosen to each time, circumstance and audience - and what He did not say was often as powerful as anything He did say. What an awesome Savior! Certainly, his precision and wisdom in handling the pressures of daily life can be attributed to his daily quiet time with the Father - something that should be a part of every believer's life.

12.5 BE FILLED WITH THE HOLY GHOST

Yielding to the move of the Spirit in our lives will have an overreaching effect on our speech, as well as any other area of our lives into which we invite Him. On the Day of Pentecost, the disciples were engaged in anointed, praise-filled speech that brought glory to God. Yes, it is true that "no man can tame the tongue" (Jas. 3:8). But that which is impossible with men is possible with God (Lk. 18:27).

A Conversation with Wisdom

12.6 A WORD ABOUT VOWS

Ecclesiastes teaches us that it is better not to make a vow to God at all, than to make one that in the end we cannot keep (Refs.). This happens because the vow was not thought through at the time it was made, and when the time comes to pay what was vowed, there is hesitation. Vows are very personal commitments between a person and their God. One example of this was the Nazarite vow, which Samson was obligated to keep from his birth (Jdg. 13:5). Hannah made a vow to return her son to the Lord in exchange for the blessing of fertility (1 Sam. 1:11). Japheth made a hasty vow, and because of his words, he was forced to commit his only daughter to lifelong virginity because of it (Jdg. 11:35-39). Paul made a vow during one of his missionary journeys (Acts 18:18).

Consider that marriage rites are vows taken before God in the presence of two or more witnesses. God takes those vows very seriously, and holds men accountable for the promises they make toward one another in His name (Pro. 20:25; Ecc. 5:4-5). Therefore, the decision to marry is best made after much prayer, practical consideration, and with as much counsel as may be available to the prospective couple.

12.7 SPEAKING UP - SPEAKING OUT

Not everyone has trouble talking too much. Some people, because of fear in their hearts (which is not of God), refrain from speaking when they know they should. This includes speaking up for the rights of the oppressed; opposing injustice; defending the poor, the fatherless and the widow. Speaking up requires boldness - and boldness comes with the anointing of the Holy Ghost and in answer to the prayers of the saints (Acts 4:31). Jesus promised His disciples that when they were dragged before the authorities and challenged about the gospel, He would give them at that very moment the words that they should speak (Lk. 21:15). There are also times when we are called to speak the hard truth to someone - but it must be done in meekness and love (Eph. 4:15).

EXAMPLES OF BOLD SPEECH

- ✓ Daughters of Zeleophad
- ✓ Esther
- ✓ Stephen
- ✓ Paul

[**Teacher's Note:** 1) Emphasize to students that the way we speak to God, to others, and even to ourselves is of critical importance to our everyday life. We can speak either death or life - faith or doubt; 2) Explain that in the Old Testament, women made vows unto God but their husbands or fathers had the right to break those vows if they felt it could not or should not be fulfilled; 3) Discuss with the class different ways they can speak up for the cause of the oppressed or speak out against injustice in their communities, city, or on the international level.]

A Conversation with Wisdom

For this cause we also, since the day we heard it, do not cease to pray and make request for you, that ye may be filled with the knowledge of his will in all spiritual wisdom and understanding, to walk worthily of the Lord unto all pleasing, bearing fruit in every good work, and increasing in the knowledge of God; strengthened with all power, according to the might of his glory, unto all patience and longsuffering with joy; giving thanks unto the Father, who made us meet to be partakers of the inheritance of the saints in light; who delivered us out of the power of darkness, and translated us into the kingdom of the Son of his love.
Paul the Apostle

CHAPTER THIRTEEN

MAKING IT PERSONAL

This final chapter is meant to bring about a period of prayerful self examination with regard to the ways godly wisdom may be applied to various situations in the student's life. Knowing the answers to the questions in this section will help the student to understand their own strengths and weaknesses, where they are in their relationship with God, and reconsider unwise patterns of living that threaten to hinder the fulfillment of divine purpose in their lives.

A Conversation with Wisdom

Ultimately, wisdom is as multifaceted as God Himself. When we are unsure about what course of action to take, we can always reflect back on the example of our Lord Jesus Christ, whose life was in perfect harmony with the Father and whose every thought, word and deed was done the right way, at the right time, and for the right reasons.

The proverbs, and principles now committed to memory are an arsenal for spiritual battles to come. They will fill your mind with precision and knowing what to do - and if we don't know what to do, we know where to go to get wisdom, and are assured that it will be ours for the asking. Remember that the beginning of wisdom is the fear of the Lord, and the conclusion of the matter is the same.

Give full answers to the questions below. Where applicable, provide verses that have helped lead you to those answers. Be prayerful about those areas in which you have difficulty, and seek out positive, right-living people in whom to confide. Make yourself available to be there to help your fellow believers as well.

CHAPTER REVIEW

1. Chapter 1. What is the fear of the Lord and why is it so important to our discussion of wisdom?

2. Chapter 2. Wisdom is likened to a woman crying aloud to people in the street. What is she saying?

3. Chapter 3. Name the four types of fools and give one characteristic of each.

4. Chapter 4. Why is delayed glory better than instant gratification?

5. Chapter 5. What is prudence? Name two people in scripture who kept good company.

6. Chapter 6. Why is good work ethic important? Why do human beings work? How does laziness lead to lack?

7. Chapter 7. What lesson did Solomon learn from pursuing all the best that life had to offer? What was his conclusion?

8. Chapter 8. What is stewardship? Why is favor with God better than money in the bank?

9. Chapter 9. What should our attitude be toward planning for tomorrow? Name two ways we may face life's challenges effectively.

10. Chapter 10. Why are advisers necessary?

11. Chapter 11. If God knows everything, why can't we just sit back and wait for Him to do everything for us?

12. Chapter 12. Name five characteristics of wise, godly speech.

GENERAL QUESTIONS

13. My relationship with God is:

    a) A source of frustration
    b) Characterized by seeking Him
    c) Seems weak when troubles come
    d) In need of a change (if so, what change?)

14. Write out John 14:26.

A Conversation with Wisdom

15. Fill in the terms that correspond to each statement.

    a) God is all knowing. (   )
    b) God is everywhere. (   )
    c) God is all powerful. (   )

16. Complete each sentence.

    a) He can enable me to accomplish anything. I would like to…
    b) He is always present with me. This assures me because…

17. Joining and staying with Jesus requires major adjustment! Read Luke 9:23-24. How do you see it?
    What kinds of adjustments have you had to make in the following areas?
    a)   Responding to Difficult Circumstances
    b)   Relationships
    c)   Actions/Overall Behavior
    d)   Thinking
    e)   Commitments-to God, to Others, to Self
    f)   Beliefs

18. What is meant by "my personal responsibility within limits?"

19. How do you feel when you must say "no" to something or someone?

20. Read Matt. 18:8-9. What was Jesus actually saying? This approach by Jesus is called a _____. He was doing this because he wanted to…

21. Psalm 119:2 teaches me…

22. In Pro. 22:3 I learn to keep it together by…

A Conversation with Wisdom

23. I must choose my friends wisely because…

[Teacher's Notes: 1) They could hand this in, but some of the answers might be of a highly personal nature, so perhaps it is better to let them present it and hold on to it for themselves. For advanced students, a more comprehensive version which asks questions about the theology of wisdom as it relates to the plan of the ages or the plan of redemption can be used, or such questions can be added to the above. The important thing is to encourage wise thinking in every day decisions.]

A Conversation with Wisdom

A Conversation with Wisdom

RECOMMENDED READING

Battle Cry For A Generation by Ron Luce, NexGen is an imprint of Cook Communications Ministries, Colorado Springs, CO 80918

Rediscovering The Kingdom by Myles Munroe, Destiny Image Publishers, Inc., Shippenburg, PA. 17257

Courage by Edwin Louis Cole, Honor, a division of Harrison House, Inc, Tulsa, Okla.

The Man In The Mirror by Patrick Morley, Zondervan Publishing House, Grand Rapids, Michigan

Breaking Strongholds in the African American Family by Dr. Clarence Walker, Zondervan Publishing House, Grand Rapids Michigan

The Pursuit of Holiness by Jerry Bridges, NavPress Publishing Group. Colorado Springs, CO

The Order of a Son by Dr. Mark Hanby, Destiny Image Publishers, Shippenburg, PA

Ray Stedman. Stedman, Ray. "Proverbs: That Men May Know Wisdom." Discovery Publishing. Blue Letter Bible. 1 Mar 1996. 2009. 2 May 2009. < http://www.blueletterbible.org/commentaries/comm_view.cfm?AuthorID=9&contentID=46&commInfo=2&topic=Proverbs >

Blue Letter Bible. "Dictionary and Word Search for sakal (Strong's 7919)". Blue Letter Bible. 1996-2009. 28 Feb 2009. < http://www.blueletterbible.org/lang/lexicon/lexicon.cfm?Strongs=H7919&t=KJV >.

Commentary on the Whole Bible by Matthew Henry
Dake's Annotated Reference Bible
E-Sword Bible Software
The McArthur Study Bible, 1997, Word Publishing. "The Book of Proverbs: Interpretive Challenges," p. 875 and notes at 31:10-31.

A Conversation with Wisdom

Nelson's Bible Dictionary
Strong's Exhaustive Concordance of the Bible
The Reformation Study Bible by R.C. Sproul
The New Scofield Study System
Vine's Expository Dictionary of Old and New Testament Words. "Wise, Skilled," 290-291. See also Strong's No. H2450.
Bible Versions: KJV, ASV

I encourage you to please consider purchasing the accompanying workbook, A Conversation with Wisdom.
ISBN 978-0-9832399-8-7

A Conversation with Wisdom

A Conversation with Wisdom

A Conversation with Wisdom

A Conversation With The Author:

One of the most exciting things about coming to the knowledge of truth is how inexhaustible it remains. More than ever, authentic Christianity in this day and time needs what is greater than mental assent and emotion. A true relationship with God must have the firm foundation of biblical truth on which to organize, build and sustain Godly character. These chapters are birthed from years of experience growing up in the inner city, and my survival as a Christian man. The precept and example of my late parents, instilled from my earliest remembrance, taught me that what I eat does not strengthen, but rather what I digest. After much thought and prayer, I feel this is the right time to add written strength and encouragement to men, women and especially the youth of our communities.

You see friend, the Kingdom of God is primarily about doing business His way. In a phrase, it is simply spiritual alignment. This book is designed to bring you the reader, into deeper experienced reality of your relationship with God. Living and moving in step with Godly wisdom, brings fulfillment to your destiny in the earth. Wise words and actions act as tools of provocation, to move you into timing and purpose. Collections of wise sayings available to us in the Holy Scriptures make us secure, steadfast and not easily moved. I invite you to dialogue with your destiny, as you read and ingest truth for your life contained in the pages of this book.

Dr. Joseph N. Williams, Sr.

A Conversation with Wisdom

A Conversation with Wisdom

Dr. Joseph N. Williams, Sr.

About the author:
Man of distinction, integrity and wisdom, developer, entrepreneur, humanitarian, musician, husband, father, preacher, mentor, educator...a few of the titles Dr. Joseph Williams operates in daily, with exemplary form. From early, humble beginnings in Brooklyn, New York, where he was born the fourth son of his father and mother, the Late Bishop John C. Williams and Dr. Kathryn J. Williams, it was evident that this spirit-filled vessel was destined for a life of public service that would reach global proportions.

A proud graduate of the New York City Public School System, and Viet Nam Vet, serving this country with dignity in the U.S. Armed Forces. His studies include concentrations in Liberal Arts, Business and Theology, along with several specialized training programs across the United States, earning a Bachelor of Arts in Economics from Brooklyn College, studies in accounting at the University of Maryland, certification from the American Institute of Banking, Masters Degrees in Religious Education and Theology, and finally, achieving Doctorates in Divinity and Sacred Theology.

The Bishop:
He was ordained in 1975, faithfully serving as Assistant Pastor, and released by Bishop Ronald H. Carter as Founder and Senior Pastor of the Apostolic Faith Assembly, now known as Christ Church International, Inc. in Jamaica, New York, and serves there to date. In 1995, Bishop Williams was consecrated to the episcopacy. To date, he continues to carry a passionate message of Christ's saving power across the globe to include Europe, Africa, Israel, Canada and the Caribbean.

A Conversation with Wisdom

A sought after conference speaker who is passionate about mentoring young men and women, in addition to ministering as an oracle of God globally. Bishop Williams believes that God desires healthy Christians spiritually and naturally, and they must be given opportunities to serve God and grow in their Christian Life. This is the trend of thought that inspired Dr. Williams to develop Harvest Development Corporation, the non-profit arm of his vision, whose mission is to advantage the disadvantaged through social and economic services. The Board of Directors comprises professional and life experienced congregants along with consultants that govern polices set forth, offering youth and adult programs and services. Additionally, Harvest Enterprises (for-profit) focuses on economic development of the membership through investment strategies and other vehicles that will produce cash flow and raise the quality of life financially for those involved

Humanitarian:

Dr. Williams' philanthropic pursuits keep him very active in the community, serving as a Chaplain for the New York City Transit Authority, as well as, Chaplain for several hospitals in the tri-state area, ministering to those in need of spiritual counsel and support. He has served on the Queens Board for Habit for Humanity and the Advisory counsel for Concerts of Prayer Greater New York, and currently serves with the Queens Network of Pastors, uniting local leadership in the public witness of Jesus Christ; is co-founder of the International Network of Churches, Ministries and Businesses, who's design is to achieve balance between ministry and business to further advance the Kingdom of God in the earth globally. Dr. Williams is proudest of his foundling, The Berean Bible Institute and School of Ministry, where the emphasis is on teaching students the content, meaning, interpretation and theology of the word of God. This is a man of inspiration and implementation, charging all he encounters to "move forward" with exuberance and passion.

A Conversation with Wisdom

Family

He shares his vision and zest for life with his wife, Carolyn Williams; a woman who has supported his efforts selflessly. Dr. Williams is the proud father of Joseph and Carla; and grandfather of three active, growing champions, Destini, Christopher and Joselyn.

A Conversation with Wisdom

A Conversation with Wisdom

A Conversation with Wisdom